Curiosities Series

South Dakota
CURIOSITIES

Quirky characters, roadside oddities & other offbeat stuff

Second Edition

Bernie Hunhoff

Guilford, Connecticut

The prices, rates, and hours listed in this guidebook were confirmed at press time. We recommend, however, that you call establishments to obtain current information before traveling.

To buy books in quantity for corporate use
or incentives, call **(800) 962–0973**
or e-mail **premiums@GlobePequot.com.**

Copyright © 2010 by Morris Book Publishing, LLC

Photos by Bernie Hunhoff unless otherwise noted.
Maps by Sue Murray copyright © Morris Book Publishing, LLC
Text design: Bret Kerr
Layout artist: Casey Shain
Project editor: John Burbidge

Library of Congress Cataloging-in-Publication data is available on file.

ISBN 978-0-7627-5868-5

ISSN 1934-5828

Printed in the United States of America

10 9 8 7 6 5 4 3

To my mom, Margaret Hunhoff,
Who besides being the mother of eight,
Plus a poet, nurse, and farmer's wife,
Made sure we could all read and write.

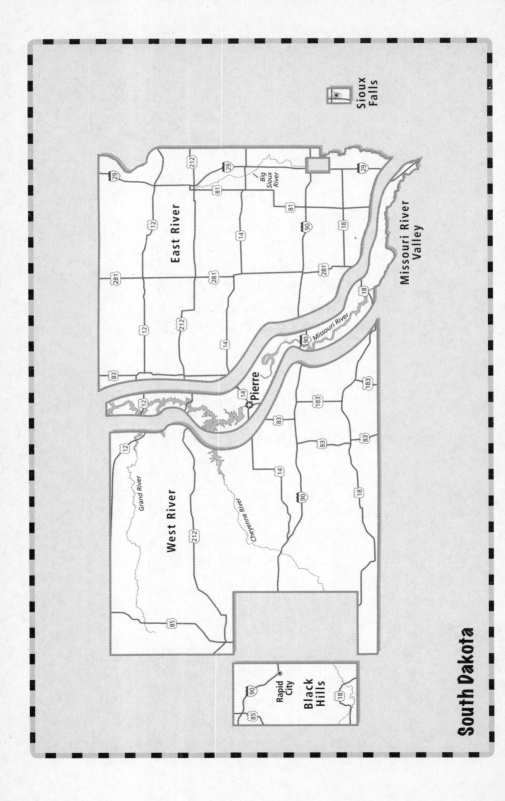

Sioux Falls

Big Sioux River

East River

Missouri River Valley

Missouri River

Pierre

Grand River

West River

Cheyenne River

Rapid City

Black Hills

South Dakota

contents

★ ★

acknowledgments

★ ★

My gratitude and thanks to everyone in South Dakota who offered tips, directions, and coffee. Special thanks to the South Dakota Tourism Department staff for friendly assistance and photographic contributions.

The book would still be in disarray, lying here and there around the office, without the help of my talented associates at *South Dakota Magazine* in Yankton. Helping with tips, photography, research, editing, and proofing were Heidi Stevens, Katie Hunhoff, Ruth Steil, Barb Hanson, Jana Lane, Andrea Maibaum, Alma Korslund, Roger Holtzmann, John Andrews, Rebecca Johnson, and Dave Jensen.

introduction

★ ★

South Dakota's old nickname, "The Land of Infinite Variety," paid homage to our mountains, lakes, badlands, and prairies. After the big mountain carving was finished in the 1930s, officials decided to emphasize the four presidents, so they passed a law declaring this to be the "Mount Rushmore State." Later, they adopted a catchy, matching motto, "Great Faces, Great Places."

At the risk of violating that law, I maintain that we still have more variety than most states—and not just in geography. We have colorful characters living interesting and even wacky lives in unusual and exotic places.

Exotic and colorful? Could we be talking about the artist in the salvage yard who made a giant bull from Cadillac bumpers? The owner of the Yankton drive-in bar, who entertains customers by flattening cans? Watertown's family of clowns? A museum made of straw? The English cottage with a thatched roof? The brewmeister who plays bagpipes?

My favorite South Dakota philosopher, the late sheepherder/writer Archie Gilfillan, pondered why our rural state produces so many characters. "Thousands of us hurl ourselves into cities like nuts into a hopper, and there, by grinding and rubbing against one another, we lose our natural form and acquire a superficial polish and a more or less standardized appearance. In the country, the nuts are not subjected to this grinding process," he surmised, so they retain their quirkiness.

By now you realize that this is not the Official South Dakota Guide to the Usual Faces and Places. It's Gilfillan's kind of travelogue. Oh, sure, Mount Rushmore and Crazy Horse and the Corn Palace are included, but so are a great many lesser-known and quite-intriguing faces and places. Nuts or not, we love them all.

But this book isn't all fun and games. There's some serious stuff. Skip past that and have a good time.

introduction

★ ★

We've divided our travel stories into five regions: East River, West River, the Missouri River Valley, the Black Hills, and Sioux Falls, our biggest city, which isn't so big that it hasn't retained a few nutty faces and places. Here are a few generic tips that might be of use when you travel all of the five regions:

- When you see a wild buffalo, stay in your car unless you can outrun a horse—because the buffalo can.
- Visit our little museums—even the smallest have something of interest. Our favorite is the exhibit of nails at the Wagner museum that supposedly came from the coffin lid of local outlaw Jack Sully.
- Get out of town after sundown. That's not a threat—it's an acknowledgment that the Dakota countryside has less "light pollution" and cleaner air than most places in America, so the stars shine amazingly bright. Do some stargazing.
- South Dakotans are proud of their state but they'll seldom brag, so don't expect them to voluntarily point you to the highest hill or the biggest plastic pheasant or the straightest road. Our stoic people are uncomfortable with superlatives—that's why this book is so necessary.
- Enjoy taverns (seasoned ground beef on a bun) and chicken noodle soup at some of the soup kitchens held during the hunting and election seasons by local churches and American Legion clubs. Hunters wear orange and politicians wear smiles. You can go as you are.

That about covers it.

I've published a magazine about life in South Dakota since 1985. Most of our readers are South Dakotans or avid travelers of the West. We featured Mount Rushmore and the Corn Palace in our first few issues, and then our travels really grew interesting as we searched for new places and faces.

introduction

We've come to expect the unexpected on every trip. And that's precisely what makes a journey so interesting—not the destination but the pleasant surprises along the way. We hope this book will make your travels more enjoyable. But don't just lazily rely on our discoveries—keep your own eyes and ears peeled for the curious and the unexpected.

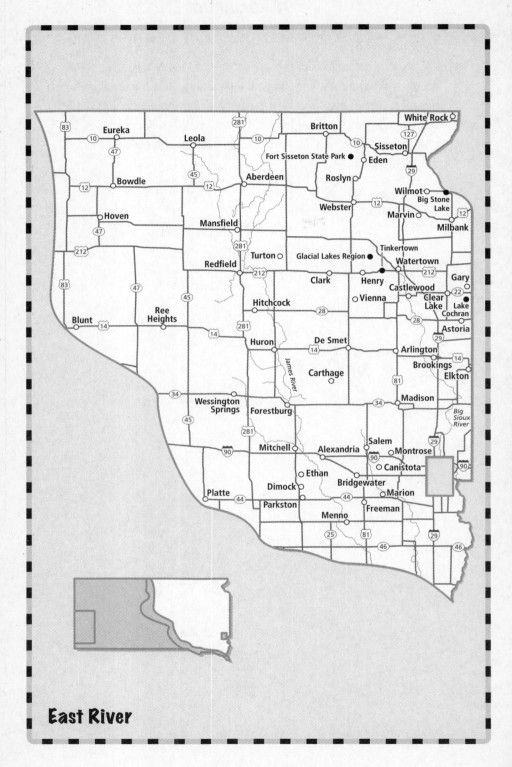

East River

1

East River

East River, as *any visitor to South Dakota soon learns, includes every-thing east of the Missouri River. Though the state's two halves are sep-arated only by a wide ribbon of water, many South Dakotans believe them to be dramatically different.*

We know South Dakotans who've traveled around the world, then came home and remarked, "You know what, people are the same everywhere." But ask them a week later about East River and West River, and they'll need an hour to point out the differences. Here's how we see it: East River has more trees, more money, and more Demo-crats, and it has fewer cowboys, fewer Indians, and no real mountains (though we do have a few big hills that exuberant pioneers misnamed).

East River has some very nice small towns and cities with a mix of industries, but it's primarily a farming culture. Most of the towns' bank-ers, preachers, and lawyers grew up on farms, and on sunny spring days they wish they could spend a day planting corn. The real surviving farmers are a modest and unassuming crowd who, though they may own land worth millions of dollars, work fourteen-hour days and drive rusty, mud-spattered pickups.

Both the city and farm citizens of East River are practical people. Their plain pickups are parked on straight streets. They farm square fields, attend modest white churches, and—as if to prove that every-thing I've written here is wrong—they also boast of some very unusual places, some of which are featured in this chapter.

Honoring Jackasses or Journalists?
Aberdeen

A stone monument to the power of the press rests in Aldrich Park in Aberdeen. According to unnamed sources, the memorial is actually there to honor Maud and Kate, two city-owned mules that hauled loads of refuse to the dump grounds and did other heavy pulling.

After they died in the 1930s, local newsman Earl Wingard decided to erect the memorial. He begged for donations with flowery prose in the local newspaper. At first the money came slowly, but Wingard kept writing stories and the public began to respond. Remember, this was the Dirty Thirties. Some people sent pool chalk, buttons, paper clips, and whatever else they had in abundance. Finally, Wingard had enough for a modest stone.

In accepting the memorial for the city, park superintendent S. H. Anderson said it should stand "as an inspiration of hope to all others that if they work hard enough and long enough . . . "

We still don't know if he was referring to the jackasses or the journalist who started it all. Does it matter? The memorial is still in the park.

Dorothy Never Was in Kansas?
Aberdeen

Dorothy tells Toto in *The Wizard of Oz,* "I've a feeling we're not in Kansas anymore!" Aberdonians know that she probably never was in Kansas. They believe her character was inspired by author Frank Baum's years as a businessman and writer in South Dakota.

Baum came to Aberdeen at age thirty-two in 1888, enamored with the Wild West and eager to make a living as a storekeeper. Despite his energetic spirit, Baum's Bazaar failed, so he got a job as a writer for the *Dakota Pioneer*. Though a bit of a know-it-all (he admonished farmers for failing to foresee hard times), the city-born Baum clearly loved the pioneer and rural experience. Literary scholars

Frank Baum created *The Wonderful Wizard of Oz.*
SOUTH DAKOTA MAGAZINE

Oz fans, big and small, love Aberdeen's Storybook Land.
SOUTH DAKOTA TOURISM

★ ★

say it inspired his creation of *The Wonderful Wizard of Oz,* which was first written as a play and then became a series of fourteen books before becoming one of Hollywood's all-time greatest movies.

Today Baum's work is still boosting Aberdeen, where a Storybook Land has been developed in Wylie Park for children, with a yellow brick road that leads to magical and mysterious places. Every June the city celebrates its literary heritage with an Oz Festival. And the Aberdeen public library has an interesting collection of Baum's books and memorabilia. You can find more information at www.aberdeen-chamber.com or call (605) 225-2860.

Maybe this will be bad for our collective ego, but if Dorothy was patterned after South Dakotans, then who among us are the cowardly lions, the timid scarecrows, the heartless tin men? One thing is certain: We have no wicked witches. Not one.

Political Bigwigs

South Dakota's best-known politician of recent times is Tom Daschle, our former U.S. senator who served as leader of the Senate. He was born in Aberdeen in 1947 and lived with his folks in a two-car garage that had been remodeled as a tiny house until 1952, when his father, Sebastian, built a two-bedroom home. George McGovern, the Democratic Party's 1972 presidential nominee, is a native of Avon and moved to Mitchell upon his retirement to hang out at the McGovern Library on the Dakota Wesleyan University campus.

Peace Be with You
Alexandria

Perhaps the most glorious and peaceful stop on I-90 is the Fatima Family Shrine, an elaborate exhibit of Catholic statuary started in 1987 by Father Robert J. Fox when he was pastor of St. Mary of Mercy Church in Alexandria.

The shrine pays tribute to the 1917 appearance of the Virgin Mary to three shepherd children at Fatima, Portugal. Mary, mother

Historic St. Mary of Mercy Church

★ ★

of Jesus, promised peace for the world if people would return to the values of the gospel and devote themselves to the rosary.

A firm believer, Father Fox created an outdoor shrine for just such devotion. It features an image of Mary modeled after the miraculous statue at Fatima. At the base is Portuguese rock and soil from the very ground by the oak tree on which Mary was seen.

Among the many other statues are representations of the three children, St. Joseph with the baby Jesus, an angel without wings (as he appeared to the children), and the fifteen mysteries of the rosary. Some statues are made of Carrara marble from Europe. The shrine is lighted at night.

The Fatima Family Shrine is adjacent to Alexandria's historic Catholic church (220 West Fifth Street), which was built of granite block a century ago. Across the street is a cloistered convent called the Monastery of Our Mother of Mercy, where fourteen Carmelite nuns work and pray for world peace and have little contact with others. We wanted to interview them, but they weren't talking. However, their brochure describes the monastery as "a hidden life of profound fruitfulness . . . "

Outside the monastery walls is a gift shop, open daily, with 10-cent holy cards, 30-cent novenas, religious tapes, and some of the fifty books Father Fox wrote to fund his shrine. For more information call Father Tom Clement at (605) 239-4833.

The Barn Straightener
Arlington

Rural artists love sagging barns, but not Arlington's Ray Christensen. He can't bear to see gravity win, so he has become a master at straightening old buildings. It started when he was working at a lumberyard in Waubay and a lady asked if anyone could straighten her barn. Ray's wife, Blanche, bragged that her husband could fix anything, so he had to try. Using cables, winches, jacks, and braces, Ray soon developed his own ways of coaxing wood beams back into place.

★ ★

Four thousand barns and buildings later, it appears that Blanche was right. But it hasn't been without sacrifice. Ray has broken nearly every rib at least once, and he's suffered several concussions.

Business boomed for many years, but now most modern farmers just tear down a barn when it starts to tilt. That's bad news for artists and barn straighteners, and for all who love old barns.

Still, East River farm country probably has more century-old barns than most places. Decide for yourself: Do you like them sagging or straight?

Ray Christensen straightens crooked barns.
CHUCK CECIL

★ ★

Farm Fashion Shows
Astoria

Hardworking East River farmers almost always wore overalls. Trygve Trooien, who farms on the east shore of Oak Lake, thinks it's a fashion craze worth preserving.

"They are cooler in the summer because they fit looser and you can always unbutton one of the buttons if you want more air circulating," he told us. Plus you've got a pliers pocket, pencil holder, and other fashion accessories too numerous to mention.

Elizabeth Johnson models a pair of overalls.

Overalls made it simple for a man to decide what to wear. "You've got your church overalls, you've got your dress overalls, you've got your town overalls, and you've got your work overalls," explains Trygve. A dress overall is for socializing in town, but it would be better than overalls you might wear to town in the afternoon to get parts or groceries. A town overall doesn't have to be as good as a dress overall, but it's better than a work overall.

When Trygve noticed that overalls were fading from store shelves, he began to stock up. His wardrobe now includes thirty-eight different styles representing twenty-six brand names like OshKosh B'Gosh, Lee, and Big Yank.

As happens with all collectors, Trygve has become an authority. When the town of Astoria celebrated its centennial in 2000, he produced an Overall Fashion Revue, a cross between a fashion show and a farm history lesson. It was so popular that he's been asked to do other shows. Trygve is the producer, and his brother, Phil, serves as announcer. They recruit young ladies to do the modeling.

If you get a chance to attend a show, don't miss it. Wear your dress overalls, and Trygve might even invite you to swagger down the runway.

The Secret Springs
Astoria

Watch for parked trucks, they say, and you'll find the best food. The same might be said of East River water. It's all good, but there must be something special about a spot along SD 28, just northwest of Astoria, where truckers and other travelers have been parking.

You'll see the tracks in the grassy ditch. They lead to Jorstad Spring, where travelers stop to fill bottles and jars with some of the freshest, cleanest water to be found in the world. Local people don't go there because they have the same good water in their kitchen taps, but out-of-towners love the place.

Long ago someone stuck a small pipe into the creek, and it has

★ ★

been gushing six gallons of good water every minute ever since. Even during the Great Drought of the 1930s, when area lakes dried up, the spring kept flowing. Some call it Astoria's Old Faithful.

A hydrogeologist confirmed that the water is unique. He credited its purity to the glacier that slid through the area 12,000 years ago, depositing so many rocks in the rough hills that it has been impossible to farm this corner of Brookings County. Since the land remains covered in native grass, few pesticides, insecticides, and fertilizers are applied. Also, the groundwater is quite young, geologically speaking, so it hasn't soaked up many underground minerals.

The water is free—and free of impurities!

★ ★

If you stop to fill a jar, don't stray into the nearby bog. Some local farmers say it's like quicksand. Cows stuck in the muck have had to be pulled out with a rope around their necks. The water's good, but it's not worth a trip to your chiropractor.

Our Worst Water Disaster
Big Stone Lake

Big Stone Lake is serene and scenic, and not nearly as busy as it was in the early years of the twentieth century when it was a major resort. Large vessels once ferried farm equipment, bags of grain, and supplies to twenty-seven ports up and down the long lake. Some excursion boats carried seventy-five passengers; a few freight boats looked like floating grocery stores.

The *Muskegon* is back on dry land.
SOUTH DAKOTA MAGAZINE

South Dakota's worst nautical disaster occurred there during a tornado in 1917 when the *Muskegon* sank with nine people aboard. When Captain Peter Luff's body was recovered, they found his pockets still full of the coins he'd collected from the riders. David Ringdahl, a passenger, said the tornado sucked the water away from the boat and tipped it on its side. Unable to find a way out, Ringdahl was about to drown when another passenger grabbed and pulled him through a window. They were the only two to survive.

Frank Douthitt, owner of the Big Stone Canning Company, later raised the *Muskegon* and used it as a lake cabin until 1985. Now it's displayed at the Big Stone County Historical Museum in Ortonville, Minnesota, just across the lake.

Tornado Alley

Bowdle

Watch for summer clouds in South Dakota, because this is tornado country. About twenty-five are spotted every year, and some have been doozies. In 1998 a twister demolished the little town of Spencer. Sixty-seven tornadoes were counted in an eight-hour period on June 24, 2003.

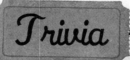

Trivia

In 1994 John Alvarez suffered brain damage in a car accident. Unable to work, he started fishing with his son. When he realized a rod and reel had magical therapeutic value, he coordinated efforts to build a wheelchair-accessible fishing hole a few miles west of town at 26331 432nd Avenue. Everybody is welcome to try his or her luck; call (605) 729-9400 for more information.

She and her horse survived a tornado ride.
SOUTH DAKOTA MAGAZINE

For fifty-one years a South Dakotan held the world record (says Guinness) for distance thrown by a tornado. Sharon Weron Fisher was a girl in Bowdle when a tornado carried her 1,300 feet. A Missouri boy beat her record by 300 feet in 2006, but there was one big difference: He was on foot. Sharon's ride was on horseback. Both she and the horse survived, and she now keeps an eye out for storms from her home in Dakota Dunes.

If Guinness had a category for "longest jump by horse and rider," we'd have the all-time champ in South Dakota.

★ ★

Woody Would'a Loved It

Britton

I'm a-chasin' my shadow out across this road map
To my wheat fields waving, to my cornfield dancing
As I go walkin' this wind keeps talkin'
This land is made for you and me.

You expect to see Woody Guthrie strumming his guitar on the hotel steps, singing "This Land Is Your Land," when you drive past miles and miles of corn and wheat, arrive in Britton, and find Don Schumaker's re-creation of a 1930s Main Street. It looks that real, even though Schumaker designed an entire old street on one big new house.

Britton's all-in-one lodging establishment

"I just always liked that period in history," he says, trying to explain why he built facades for a saloon, hotel, bank, auto dealer, and gas station on a single house. Parked out front are some of his 1928–1931 vintage cars and pickups, including a Model A Roadster.

Schumaker and his wife, Norma, opened their unusual house at 1003 First Street as the Apple Valley Bed and Breakfast for visitors to their Glacial Lakes community of 1,400 in extreme northeast South Dakota. Call the Schumakers at their furniture store (605-448-5312 or 448-2223) for information on the B&B or Britton.

Trivia

One of America's five continental divides cuts across the northeast corner of South Dakota. From the divide (which consists of a long range of scenic hills), water flows northerly to Canada's Hudson Bay or southerly to the Missouri River and the Gulf of Mexico. The city of Britton sits on the divide, but there's no specific geographic boundary so it's hard to figure out exactly which side you're on. It's like modern politics—the higher you get, the more you have to straddle.

Politics and the great divide

★ ★

180 Steps to a Prairie View
Brookings

When you visit the South Dakota State University campus in Brookings, enjoy the ice cream made by dairy science students and then work off the calories by climbing the 165-foot Campanile that was built in 1929 thanks to the generosity of Charles Coughlin. He was

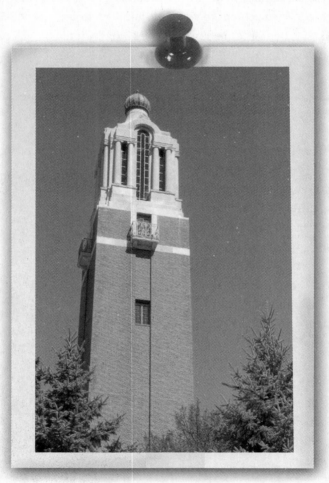

The Campanile, our prairie lighthouse
SOUTH DAKOTA TOURISM

a Carthage farm kid who graduated from the school and went on to success as a Wisconsin industrialist.

The limestone and redbrick tower has become a Brookings landmark and a symbol for the state's largest higher education institution. Due to flashing red aircraft-warning lights atop the tower, it is not only a skyline steeple by day, but also a beacon, like a lighthouse on the prairie, for students returning to campus on Sunday nights. Many collegiate couples shared a first kiss, or got engaged, on the steps. For years it was tradition for the homecoming committee to spend a night at the top.

Anyone with the gumption to climb the Campanile may go to Tompkins Alumni Office across the street for a key. If you're successful, you get a coupon for a free ice-cream cone and a certificate signed by SDSU president David Chicoine, who also holds the esteemed title of Chief Bell Ringer.

Go, Flowers!
Brookings

If flowers were as popular as football in American culture, South Dakota State University would be the envy of the Fighting Irish, the Cornhuskers, the Bruins, and all the other collegiate bigwigs. And the Rose Bowl of that world would be McCrory Gardens, the prettiest seventy-acre patch of land you'll ever see.

Flower fans would fly to Brookings from both coasts when McCrory's 1,000 varieties of roses bloomed or the maple leaves turned red. The aroma of grilled hot dogs at tailgate garden parties would blend beautifully with the fragrances of hollyhocks and tulips.

Instead of wanting to see Disneyland, young Johnny would beg to explore the Children's Maze. "Dad, it's over 1,100 feet of hedges!" he'd whine. And his big sis would say, "Mom, when I get married, I want to have my wedding in McCrory Gardens. I don't care if Dad does know somebody at Wrigley Field."

SDSU's horticulture department started the ornamental gardens

★ ★

in 1965 as a research plot, and also to educate and entertain visitors. Yes, if it were a football team, it would be on the front pages every season because McCrory's is routinely ranked all-American by national flower and nursery associations.

Fortunately for us, flowers have not replaced football. McCrory Gardens is not trampled and crowded. Even in peak colors, it's quieter than 4:00 a.m. on a Division I football field. Best of all, there's no admission, no parking fees, no waiting in line, and no stale popcorn or spilled beer.

Don't spread the word.

For information on the Brookings area, visit www.brookings chamber.org or call (605) 692-6125.

Brookings's all-American flower garden
SOUTH DAKOTA MAGAZINE

★ ★

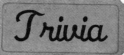

Trivia

While at SDSU in Brookings, ask for directions to the Dairy Building, where students create the ice cream. They've perfected a hundred flavors. Enjoy a cone and take some with you—along with cheese, yogurt, butter, and cheese bread. For information call the alumni office at (888) SDJACKS.

Hobo Day, an Anomaly at SDSU

Brookings

There's only one word to describe it: anomaly (*Webster:* deviation from the common rule; irregularity). You pay dearly to send your pride and joy off to South Dakota State University—a seemingly respectable institution staffed by concerned and well-spoken faculty in a conservative, tree-shaded prairie city—and in a few weeks that son or daughter is cavorting on the street in tattered clothes like a common bum. And the administration approves!

Yes, Hobo Day is one of life's rare anomalies. Rarely do we have an opportunity to throw convention aside, with the university president leading the parade.

Hobo Day is our biggest university's biggest event. And it has a rich history. State lost its first two games of the 1912 football season by big margins, so morale was already low on campus when students were told that they had to scrap their traditional homecoming celebration—the Nightshirt Parade, in which the student body donned pajamas and nighties and performed a snake dance.

The administration thought the Nightshirt Parade was undignified for female students, so when a Hobo Day was proposed, officials jumped at the notion. Hobos have been a colorful and

★ ★

unconventional anomaly at SDSU ever since. The famous Bummobile was donated in 1939. Weary Willy was introduced in 1950, and Dirty Lil showed up in 1976.

State beat Yankton College 6–3 on the first Hobo Day; since then, the school has amassed a 56-35-5 homecoming record. Not bad for a bunch of bums.

The Bummobile, a 1912 Model T, chauffeurs SDSU royalty.
SOUTH DAKOTA MAGAZINE

Hungry? Catch the Goosemobile
Canistota

A brown cardboard box appears nearly the same color as a fine pumpkin pie, but it doesn't taste the same. So it is with meat and poultry, according to Tom Neuberger, creator of the Goosemobile. He believes a bird that roams free, dirt-scratching and insect-pecking on the open range, is going to taste better than one raised in a 12-inch-square wire pen with antibiotics and hormones and other chemicals.

That theory got a severe test in 1984 when Tom and his wife, Ruth, fattened 3,500 geese the natural way and found themselves without a market. They decided to process the geese and hit the road

Tom Neuberger, on the road with the Goosemobile

★ ★

in a refrigerated bus, selling town to town. The Goosemobile was such a success that they've been traveling South Dakota ever since. Now they offer the Christmas goose along with natural organic beef, pork, goat, ostrich, goose eggs, down comforters, and feather pillows. Try finding all that at your local Cheapo-Mart.

Obviously, if the Goosemobile meats didn't taste better than store-bought, the Neubergers would be home by the fireplace on December nights. Instead, they're crisscrossing South Dakota (they visited 185 communities one year), greeting loyal customers by their first names and proving that there is more than one way to survive on a farm.

For a Goosemobile schedule or to shop at their farm by Canistota (southwest of Sioux Falls), call the Neubergers at (605) 296-3314.

A History of Pain Relief

Canistota

Dakota farmer Amon Ortman found that his hands had a healing touch on friends and family members, and soon the news spread. Each day as he returned from his fields in the 1920s, someone was always waiting to have him massage and manipulate a sore neck or back. He had them take a seat—on a wagon tongue, buggy seat, or bucket. Eventually he surmised that the Sitting-up Technique aided the healing.

Amon's brother, Noah, began to help him provide treatments. In 1929 they opened a chiropractic office in Canistota. Since then four generations of Ortman doctors have treated more than three million patients. Several hundred a day come to the clinic in the little town, seeking relief for muscular aches and pains.

The Ortman Clinic's constant flow of patients has kept Canistota (population 610) alive. It has more restaurants, motels, and gift shops than most cities five times its size. The clientele is an interesting mix of folks from across the region and includes many Amish people, who arrive wearing their trademark black and mix with other visitors at the local shops and cafes.

Amon's and Noah's children, grandchildren, and great-grandchildren have continued the Sitting-up Technique developed on buggy seats, but the nine current doctors all studied and earned degrees in modern chiropractic medicine as well.

What town of 600 has profited so much from pain, and yet done so much to kill it?

The clinic number is (605) 296-3431; the Web address is www.ortmanclinic.com.

Museum Made of Straw
Carthage

Huff and puff all you like—you won't blow this straw house down. The citizens of Carthage wanted a unique replacement for the historic Wiley House Museum when it was condemned as unsafe. After much research the Carthage Historical Society settled on the notion of building America's only straw-bale museum in 1999.

The museum made of 1,300 straw bales
CAMPBELL ORIGINAL STRAW BALE MUSEUM

★ ★

Local farmers donated 1,300 straw bales for the 6,000-square-foot wood-frame structure, and volunteers did the rest. Though straw construction is common in some parts of the world, it was new to Carthage, so they bought a book and "read up."

The bales are framed by wood, giving the interior a rustic look that befits a museum of pioneer life, and stucco was applied to a chicken-wire covering. The stairway of the Wiley House was reconstructed inside.

The Campbell Original Straw Bale Museum (206 East Main Street) is open year-round. A Straw Bale Days celebration is held every July, featuring games, food, parades, a straw-bale toss, and a cow plop (don't ask). For more information call (605) 772-4716.

An Unforgotten Grave

Castlewood

Frontier winters were especially hard on women and children. East of Castlewood, homesteader Per Gustav Erikson lost his wife, Ida May, and their baby girl to diphtheria in 1886. Because the snow was so deep and the ground frozen solid, the grieving young settler kept the rough-hewn coffins in a shed until spring, when he dug two graves and buried his family above the Hidewood Valley. He probably had no money for a permanent marker, but he planted blue flag flowers (cousin to the iris) in the loose soil. Then he sold his claim and left.

Forty-five years later, Floyd Haug discovered the graves. "I was fixing fence on May 10 and I saw two perfect rectangles of blue flowers," he said. With a little research he discovered Erikson's sad story. More than a century later, the flowers still bloom every May, making perfect blue rectangles over two lonesome graves.

The graves are on a high ridge about a half mile west of the Castlewood rest area along I-29 in the historic Hidewood Valley, so named because Indians involved in bloody conflicts with white settlers in Minnesota hid in its thick oak trees in 1862.

24

Mashed Potato Wrestling
Clark

Potato farming was once important to Clark County. What a proud heritage: The farmers fed thousands of people and were good stewards of the land. Now the people of Clark show due respect and appreciation for that history every August by wrestling one another in a huge pit of mashed potatoes.

They call it good, clean fun. When it does get messy, the volunteer firemen "hose off" the wrestlers.

Naturally, there's lots of potato humor. What do you call a baby potato? A small fry. And how do you appease a mad potato? Why, butter him up, of course.

Even ESPN has covered Clark's potato wrestling.
CLARK'S FLOWER AND GIFT

The spectacle is good publicity for the little town. ESPN, ABC, and other major sports media have squeezed it into their schedules on occasion because Potato Day always falls in dull August, in between the end of the NBA playoffs and the start of the NFL season.

Maybe you're too cultured for potato wrestling. You lean more toward the artistic? Well, Clark also hosts a potato sculpting and design contest. A dentist once carved a giant tooth, and the hardware store owner made a wrench, pliers, and hammer. The culinary arts are also practiced; cooks compete for the best dish and recipe. Of course, potato must be the main ingredient.

For information on the next Potato Day, call (605) 532-5685.

LTDs on Parade
Clark

Kenny Bell insists he's not an artist, just a fellow who makes "conversation starters." But isn't that what good art does?

Bell doesn't do pretty sunsets and waterfalls. He plants a bunch of rusty, bent culverts in the ground and calls it a tribute to the Gulf War. He leans wood telephone poles at an angle and calls them *The Nine Spirits.* He collects seven identical 1976 Ford LTDs, parks them in a row, and calls them *The Parade.*

And like many good artists, Bell lets the work speak for itself. His big, abstract outdoor art gets people talking, but he keeps mum. His wife, Sandy, says the collections are just his way of expressing himself.

Bell planned to explode some giant fuel tanks a few years ago. That really got people talking—including state safety authorities, who came by for some conversation. They said they wished he wouldn't.

Look for Bell's outdoor art in the fields just west of Clark along US 212.

Kenny Bell's LTDs on parade

Trivia

While in Clark, stop by Desnoyers Hardware (123 North Commercial Street), a family business since 1892. The proprietor, H. T. Desnoyers, is the town's top ambassador—he knows all the natives and their dogs, he's the first to greet strangers, and he hands out gold-plated coins to kids.

★ ★

Little Fellow's Grave
Clark

If you're lucky enough to reach Heaven, greet your family and friends
first. But with eternity on your hands, you'll then want to expand
your acquaintances. We suggest you watch for Big Bill Chambers and
a lad known in South Dakota as Little Fellow. They'll likely be hanging
out near a railroad track. (Would it be Heaven without trains?)

Big Bill was a brakeman on the Chicago & Northwestern when the
railroad was extended into Clark County. Little Fellow's parents ran a
kitchen for the railroaders. He was a sickly lad who loved trains, so he
and Big Bill became good friends. The railroader told the boy about
America's big cities and his adventures, and the two exchanged
waves every time the train whistled past the boy's tar-paper shack.

Sadly, Little Fellow died in 1890, and his parents put a very modest
marker on his grave. They were devastated when they had to move
away to the next railroad job, but they felt better when Big Bill said
he'd watch over Little Fellow's grave. Big Bill was promoted to con-
ductor, but he was never too busy for Little Fellow. He directed work
crews to keep the grass clipped around his friend's stone marker, and
he never passed by without wanting to wave. He and his crew always
stopped the train on Memorial Day for a visit and a prayer. Big Bill,
the gruff and busy railroader, visited the grave for forty-one years,
until he died in 1931.

Then Vince Ford, Bill's son-in-law, took responsibility and held an
annual service. When Vince died, other family members kept up the
tradition. Eventually the Clark Rotary Club "adopted" Little Fellow,
and the Rotarians have held Memorial Day services at the grave site
since the 1950s.

When train service to Clark was discontinued, the railroad left the
section of track by the grave as a tribute to Little Fellow. The grave
site (6 miles east of Clark along SD 212) is maintained and open to
the public. Visitors are especially welcome at the annual Memorial
Day service. Visit www.clarksd.com for details.

★ ★

Corden, South Dakota?
Clark

You won't find Corden on a map, but avid readers of the Carl Wilcox mystery series know the place better than Rapid City or Sioux Falls.

Harold Adams, a successful Minnesota author, spent his boyhood summers in Clark. He bases some of his stories on local people, events, and places, but he never uses real names and refers to Clark as Corden. Carl Wilcox, his main character, is a jailbird and small-time troublemaker who luckily lands a job as a private investigator during the Great Depression.

You'd think the people of Clark would be eager to guess the identity of characters and places, but few admit to reading the series, which includes such titles as *The Ditched Blonde, A Way with Widows,* and *The Man Who Was Taller Than God.*

"Too racy!" one lady told us.

How does she know?

Where the Pavement Ends
Clear Lake

Maybe every successful rodeo got its start from a cowboy's dream. Certainly, that's how America's most unique rodeo arena was built. E. W. Weisel was on horseback in 1936, gazing at a circular valley on his ranch north of Clear Lake, when he had a vision. "I dreamed it," he said years later. "I dreamed it was all there, with horses and cattle and the people all laughing and having a good time."

At the bottom of the valley was a duck pond. Weisel drained the water, made a wobbly corral from corn cribbing, found a few wild broncs, and recruited some cowboys to put on a show. Hundreds of people came to watch, so he got a bank loan and built a real arena with lights. The Crystal Springs Rodeo soon grew to become one of the most popular events on the pro rodeo circuit.

Weisel spent lots of money, but very little of it on road improvements. Instead he advertised the cow trail to the rodeo grounds as

★ ★

"Where the pavement ends and the West begins!" And he never built bleachers. In his vision, he saw people sitting on the hillside, and that's the way it is today. Cowboys consider it America's most natural rodeo bowl, so take along a lawn chair or pillow if you don't like green grass stains on your white pants.

The Crystal Springs Rodeo is held in late June every year. The cow trail has been graveled, but not paved. Call (605) 874-2996 for more information. The nearby city of Clear Lake celebrates rodeo weekend with a buffalo-burger feed, snowmobile races on grass, a citywide rummage sale, a car show, and other festivities.

The old duck pond
CRYSTAL SPRINGS RODEO

Big Trees on the Prairie
De Smet

Although Walnut Grove, Iowa, got far more publicity from the popular *Little House on the Prairie* television series, many of the Ingalls family's homesteading experiences happened in De Smet.

Despite the Hollywood snub, fans of the long-running series still find their way to the real little town on the prairie. And they're never disappointed. The community has carefully preserved two houses occupied

Old cottonwoods are a living legacy of the Ingalls family.
SOUTH DAKOTA TOURISM

by Charles and Caroline and their kids, along with fourteen other historic buildings mentioned in Laura Ingalls Wilder's many books.

There's even a living reminder of the Ingalls family: A small grove of cottonwood trees planted by Pa still thrives by the big slough. The Ingallses' 160-acre homestead, which cost Pa just $16 in filing fees, has been restored to its nineteenth-century look. In the summer horse-and-wagon tours are available at a nearby visitor center.

The little town stages a Laura Ingalls Wilder outdoor pageant on weekends in July. For pageant information call (800) 880-3383.

Where Ducks Swim above Barns
De Smet

Nobody in Kingsbury County figured they needed flood insurance when Lake Thompson was just a big slough, full of cattails, waterfowl, and frogs. But in the 1980s the water started to rise and spread, and by 1990 it was classified as the largest natural lake in the state. (Only the man-made lakes on the Missouri are bigger.)

As the lake grew to 20,000 acres, it flooded many families' homes and farms. Some farmers moved to town or left the area altogether. Others made proverbial lemonade from the rising water and opened fishing resorts above their flooded fields and barns.

Meadows and valleys where cows and sheep happily grazed have proved equally friendly to walleye and pike, which love the shallow inlets and bays. Beef is still king in Kingsbury County, but farmers are adjusting—and they appreciate the fact that a walleye will never jump a pasture fence, unless the fence is 10 feet underwater.

Lake Thompson is near De Smet at the southern end of a chain of glacial lakes that stretch across northeast South Dakota. Call the Glacial Lakes Association at (800) 224-8860 for fishing and lodging information.

Squeaky Cheese Curds
Dimock

Dimock Dairy's headquarters is a clean little white building on the east edge of town. At 5:00 a.m. daily, nine workers arrive to make cheese as it was done when local dairy farmers started the plant in 1931.

Somehow the little cooperative has escaped corporate agriculture's takeovers and megamergers that have swallowed or closed almost every other small cheese plant in the region. Dimock's cheese is delivered to grocery stores, sold in school vending machines, and shipped to loyal customers across the nation.

Local farmers still own the plant, even though most of them no longer milk cows. The entire town is the dairy's marketing team: Everyone boasts of the cheese, spreading the word far and wide.

Judy Moege, a veteran cheese maker, recommends the Colby, but customers have many favorites, among them cheddar, Monterey Jack, Ko-Jack, and salsa. Moege says visitors often stop for fresh cheese curds, which she calls "precheese," or cheese that hasn't yet been blocked and aged. It squeaks like bubble gum when fresh—but the squeak is gone by the time it gets to a store shelf or travels through the mail.

Call (605) 928-3833 to order by phone, or stop by the old dairy's front office on 400 Main Street for the squeak. There's no extra charge.

Cheese curds, booyah and beer,
That's what I like to hear.
I may be kinda pokey,
But I say "okey-dokey!"
To cheese curds, booyah and beer.
—from Belgians in Heaven

★ ★

That's a Lot of Bull(head)
Eden

Guinness doesn't track bullhead lore, but regular customers of Club Eden (322 Broadway) are confident that a record was set there years ago by a nameless patron who sat down and ate seventeen.

Obviously the hungry stranger had a strong stomach—but part of the credit must go to the Eden chefs, who know just how to prepare the much-maligned fish. Many anglers scorn bullheads because they are dark and whiskery, with sharp spines that sting with a beelike poison. Still, in the Glacial Lakes country of northeast South Dakota, the "bottom feeder" is so popular that Club Eden has a bullhead fish fry on Friday nights. It's "all you can eat," but nobody has come close to the record in years.

Club Eden is famous for fish fries and polka dancing.
DAVID JENSEN

Bullheads are plentiful in the Eden area; the state's largest bullhead (three pounds, eleven ounces) was caught in 1993 at Big Stone Lake, 35 miles away. If you're not a bullhead aficionado, the Glacial Lakes also have walleye, bass, and crappie.

Friday nights aren't the only hot time at Club Eden; it's open seven days a week. On Sunday afternoons customers move the pool table aside for a polka dance. Weekday mornings are devoted to whist and pinochle games. And free food is served Thursday nights, courtesy of local businesses. Call (605) 486-4144 to check on activities at Club Eden.

Helen's Spoons
Ethan

The furthest thing you'll ever find from a chain restaurant is Cook's Inn, a pleasant respite on Ethan's main street. Ethan (population 310) doesn't have a grocery store, so proprietor Marilyn Thill stocks a corner of the cafe with necessities for the elderly who can't drive to Mitchell or Parkston. When she's not busy in the kitchen, she makes Mouse Dolls out of fabric and pop bottles. Her front counter has bowls of complimentary peanuts, cookies, and candies—just help yourself.

Hanging on the back wall is farmwife Helen Garvis's spoon collection. Mrs. Garvis collected about a hundred spoons from all over the world. There's a lobster spoon, an Elvis guitar spoon, a Bethlehem spoon, and, of course, a Corn Palace spoon. After she died at age ninety-four in 2006, her household items were auctioned. Marilyn thought it would be a shame to see the collection split up by antiques dealers, so she bought them all.

When the late farmwife's friends and relatives stop at Cook's Inn for a burger, they see the collection and say excitedly, "Well, you've got Helen's spoons!"

"Yes, I do," Marilyn proudly replies.

For more information call (605) 227-4420.

Gut Deutsche Dining!

It should be no *über-raschung* that South Dakota has kuchen factories, dachshund races, schmeckfests, and other Germanic foods and fun. Forty percent of South Dakotans claim German ethnicity. Next largest are the Norwegians (15 percent), the Irish (10 percent), and Native Americans (once 100 percent in these parts and now 8 percent). Germanfests often focus on beer, brats, and other culinary delights. Here are three favorites:

Sioux Falls: Our state's largest city holds a Germanfest every September in Falls Park West featuring dachshund races, accordion music, beer, and brats. Call (605) 274-2423.

Eureka: This little town near the North Dakota border is considered the Kuchen Capital. Its September Schmeckfest has music, a fair, pioneer demonstrations, a tractor pull, beer, and brats. Call (605) 577-6654.

Deadwood: The Black Hills gambling mecca opens its Main Street for an Oktoberfest that includes wiener dog races, beer barrel games, and free brats. Call (800) 999-1876.

Freeman: The community of Germans-from-Russia serves Mennonite meats, salads, soups, and desserts to 1,000 people per night over two weekends in March or early April at a gala celebration known as Schmeckfest. Call (605) 925-4689 for dates and details.

Beer and brats are staples at Sioux Falls' Germanfest.

Enjoy Kuchen: It's the Law

Eureka

South Dakotans have cracked down on certain addictive substances, like tobacco and alcohol, but kuchen use quadrupled in 2000 when the South Dakota legislature voted it our state dessert.

For non-German readers, we should explain that kuchen is an Old German sweet cake made with dough and any filling you can find in the fridge, garden, or kitchen cabinet—rhubarb, peaches, pumpkin, apples, or even chocolate and peanut butter. Very *gut* stuff when safely consumed in moderation.

Eureka women sweetened up the legislators until they agreed to pass the "kuchen bill." The Czechs tried to amend the measure to include kolaches, and the Norwegians filibustered for krumkake. Yes, it was a big political brouhaha, but never bitter or hard to swallow; most of the senators gained ten pounds or more in that forty-day legislative session.

Afterwards the Eureka women went home and joyfully started several kuchen-making businesses. There they bake the state dessert (up to 200 kuchens a day) and other sweets with less political weight— like caramel rolls and Pfepperneuse cookies, which might have been the state cookie, but the speaker of the house couldn't pronounce *Pfepperneuse,* so that idea soon crumbled.

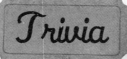

Trivia

The Glacial Lakes region covers most of the state's northeast quadrant. For information on outdoor activities and amenities, call the Glacial Lakes Association at (800) 244-8860.

★ ★

World's Fastest Stuntwoman
Eureka

Only one South Dakota woman has ever set a world record by driving 618 miles per hour in a hydrogen-powered dragster. (To keep the record straight, no South Dakota male has even come close.)

But that's only a speed bump on Kitty O'Neill's résumé. She was an Olympic diver, a skilled pianist, and one of Hollywood's most

South Dakota's fastest woman

★ ★

successful and attractive stuntwomen—all despite losing her hearing at five months of age from a high fever brought on by measles. "A handicap is not a defeat," she says, "but a challenge to be conquered." After retiring to Eureka, she took that message to local schools, reaching out especially to students who are deaf.

O'Neill was a look-alike stunt double for the famous actress Sally Fields when both were in the prime of their careers, so she worked in *Smokey and the Bandit* and other major films. All this has earned her a corner space in the Eureka Pioneer Museum (1210 North Lake Drive)—and that's where most of her memorabilia now hangs, because when she moved to town a few years ago, she decided she didn't want Hollywood paraphernalia on her living room walls. "I don't like to be famous," she said. "I'm actually a very private person. There were a lot of phony people in California, but not here."

Eureka's other celebrity is Al Neuharth, the famed journalist who founded *USA Today* in Florida. Neuharth still owns his childhood home in the little McPherson County town, and he often returns for extended visits and shows up for conversation in the coffee shops.

Trivia

Eureka is a modest, delightful German-American town where some residents still speak with an accent. A picturesque swimming lake borders the west side of town. Be sure to enjoy the local breakfast sausage, and, of course, visitors are welcome at the kuchen bakeries. For information on the town, call the Community Development Company at (605) 284-2130.

No Pessimism Please

A lone gravestone stands in a field across the highway from the Eureka Pioneer Museum. The inscription reads RIP: HERE LIES THE PAST. In a ceremony led by Al Neuharth, one of the USA's best-known newspapermen, the townspeople symbolically buried all their pessimism a few years ago. Please don't say it was a dumb idea.

Eureka buried its negativity 6 feet under.
KATIE HUNHOFF

★ ★

"Angel's Food" Sold on Highway 34
Forestburg

"When one has tasted watermelon," said Mark Twain, "he knows what the angels eat."

Some of the sweetest watermelons in America grow in the James River bottomlands between Mitchell and Huron. And the very best melon fields lie in a 12-mile square between Forestburg and Woonsocket. Sand Creek runs through the farms, and the growers believe something in the sandy soil adds sweetness to their melons.

Forestburg watermelons sell better than hotcakes in grocery stores across the region, but true fans head for SD 34 south of Huron in late summer and thump their own at roadside stands run by the farm families.

Actually, thumping is a layman's test of ripeness. Experienced growers can judge ripeness from 10 feet away. But customers needn't worry: The Forestburg farmers would turn red with embarrassment if they sold you a melon that was green inside.

Trouble Finding a Dance Partner?
Fort Sisseton

So the ladies avoid you at dances? They look the other way when you approach? And when you tap them on the shoulder, they insist they must visit the powder room?

We advise you to attend the annual military costume ball (military or pioneer attire) at the Fort Sisseton Festival, held the first weekend every June. Dancers there are expected to abide by the standards set forth in the 1860 *New York Etiquette Book*:

Of special importance is the proper way to request a dance. The gentleman approaches a lady, makes a slight bow from the waist, and says, "Will you do me the honor to dance with me?" or "May I have the honor of this dance?" If she is not free, he asks when she is not engaged, and if she'll do him the honor

*of dancing with him then. A lady must never refuse a dance
without a good reason, and she should accept the next available
dance graciously.*

If you can't get a dance at Fort Sisseton, you need to rethink
your hygiene. Still, all won't be lost. The festival also has draft-horse
pulls, fiddlers, melodramas, a medicine show, a fur traders' rendezvous, Native American dancing, a Dutch oven cook-off, and cannon
shooting.

Fort Sisseton is south of Britton in northeast South Dakota. Call
the park office at (605) 448-5474 for more information.

Fort Sisseton, built in 1864, has been restored.
SOUTH DAKOTA TOURISM

★ ★

Before Tractors There Was Haar's

Freeman

Thirty-five years before John Deere ever made a tractor (or even a T-shirt), the Haar family was selling the company's steel plow. It all began when Fred Haar emigrated from Russia and opened a farm machinery store in the new town of Freeman. The only horsepower he sold had four legs and burned hay.

John Deere's horse-drawn steel moldboard plow was a hit with his customers because the rich, black prairie soil stuck to other plows,

Haar's John Deere store in the 1930s
FRED HAAR CO.

44

while it "scoured," or slid off, the polished steel of the Deere plow. In 1917 the Deere family bought the Waterloo tractor company and stuck their name on it. Today the Deere company puts the leaping deer logo on everything from tricycles and pink caps to toy trucks and handkerchiefs—and you can find it all at Haar's farm store in Freeman, along with a plow if you need one.

The John Deere logo ranks with Coca-Cola and Harley Davidson as the most popular in America, so you've probably stumbled on some Deere memorabilia at chain stores everywhere. But if you feel awkward buying John Deere items in a box store that sells lawn chairs from China and towels from Taiwan, then you're the type that appreciates Haar's, which is now run by Fred's great-grandson Jim, and his great-great-grandson Al.

It's easy to spot their big store on the northern outskirts of Freeman (615 North US 81) because rows and rows of gleaming green tractors and combines are parked out front. Inside you'll find a modern farm implement dealership stocked with belts, pulleys, sprockets, blades, and bolts. The front of the store is devoted to John Deere merchandise, and the south wall is a museum of Haar family and Freeman pictures and memorabilia. There seems to also be a pleasant fragrance of clean grease, oil, and steel, but that may be a figment of the imagination.

"We think we're the nation's oldest John Deere dealership in the same family," says Jim. That should be on a T-shirt (with a deer, of course). Learn more about the Haar family's tractor history at www .fredhaar.com or phone (605) 925-4241.

The Origins of American Chislic
Freeman

You can order a decent steak in North Dakota or Nebraska, and Iowa's pork chops are tasty. But chislic is unique to southeast South Dakota.

★ ★

A Russian treat on a stick

Chislic is bite-size chunks of lamb on a stick, seasoned and deep-fat fried or grilled. The delicacy's arrival in America has been traced to John Hoellwarth, who arrived in Hutchinson County in the 1870s from Crimea in southern Russia, where shashlyk (skewered meat cubes grilled on a fire) was popular.

The town of Freeman is considered the chislic capital. Travel more than 30 or 40 miles away from there, and people can hardly pronounce it, let alone cook it.

Not even the Russians of Crimea could take chislic more seriously than Papa's Restaurant in Freeman (1121 South US 81), where they sell up to 3,000 sticks a week; it's a standing lunch special. "Three sticks or six?" asks the waitress. Papa's serves five varieties: original, barbecue, lemon pepper, garlic, and a house specialty that's marinated in olive oil, lemon juice, and soy sauce. Call Papa's beforehand to make sure they haven't sold out (605-925-4496).

Did Jesse Jump the Gulch?

Garretson

Real cowboys spend lots of time alone. But they occasionally enjoy a good argument—especially one involving horses and outlaws and banks.

Years ago, cowboys might have argued over whether a horse could outrun a coyote. Later, a popular topic was whether a horse could outrun an automobile. Topics come and go, but one particular issue has been kicked around by cowboys and other equine experts since September of 1876 when Jesse James and brother Frank rode through the Sioux Falls vicinity after robbing the First Federal Bank in Northfield, Minnesota. The outlaws were trying to distance themselves from a posse when they reached the rough breaks around Split Rock Creek north of Garretson.

As the story goes, Jesse was riding on the east side of the creek, while Frank was on the west side. As the posse closed in on Jesse, he supposedly spurred his horse—a nearly blind old nag that he'd stolen earlier in the day—and jumped the 18-foot chasm to join Frank on the west bank and make his escape.

Jesse wouldn't have had to worry about parole or prison food if the leap had failed. He and the horse would have almost surely met their Maker in the rocky, deep creek 70 feet below.

Historians have verified that the James brothers' escape route included a stretch of Split Rock Creek, but it's impossible to say whether or not Jesse actually jumped across what's now called Devil's Gulch.

The mystery makes for a good argument, and it inspired local officials to create a small tourism trade around the supposed jump. Visitors can ride the Jesse James Pontoon (call 605-594-2255 for reservations), hike several trails in Palisades State Park, enjoy the Devil's Fall and Devil's Stairway, and view the 1930s WPA architecture in the stone buildings, bridges, and walls of Split Rock Park. A local museum has Jesse James materials, and regional thespians perform in the Jesse James Opera House on occasion.

★ ★

Every June the town of Garretson hosts Jesse James Days, and, naturally, one of the top topics of conversation is whether a man and a horse can leap 18 feet across the creek. We'll never know for certain, but you are entitled to your opinion. That's part of the Cowboy Code in these parts. Bank robbery, by the way, is now a violation of the code.

Whoa! Jesse has his doubters.

★ ★

A Small Town's Dream Comes True

Gary

The town of Gary is proof that it never hurts to hope. Gary was home to the state's School for the Blind in the first half of the twentieth century, but officials moved the school to Aberdeen in the 1950s, leaving an empty campus of historic buildings. What do you do with big, old dormitories and classrooms in a town of 200? The townspeople sadly watched them deteriorate.

Meanwhile, Joe Kolbach left the little South Dakota town of Howard while still in his teens and traveled to the West Coast, where he found work in the fledgling wind energy business. He soon became a successful international entrepreneur, but he never forgot his South Dakota roots, and eventually he started companies in Howard and in Gary.

Joe and his wife, Tina, were living near Gary when he sold Energy Maintenance Services in 2007 for millions of dollars. The couple decided they wanted to stay in the area to raise their family, so they asked the community what they'd like to see happen. It didn't take their neighbors long to answer: Could you do something with the blind school?

If you want something done, ask an entrepreneur. The Kolbachs enlisted the help of local contractors, literally rolled up their own sleeves, and went to work in 2008. First off, they chased out the pigeons and raccoons. Within a year, the campus reopened as the Buffalo Ridge Resort and Business Center, a charming retreat destination with a small hotel, campgrounds, meeting spaces, an outdoor plaza, and other amenities.

And could we rebuild Lake Elsie? someone asked. The little lake on Lac Qui Parle Creek had been closed for many years because a child had drowned there. After the family of the child gave their approval, the Kolbachs bulldozed a new hole for the lake, and now it's popular with swimmers, sunbathers, and anglers.

Gary is a tidy town on the South Dakota/Minnesota border, with several nightspots and interesting shops. Lake Cochrane, one of the cleanest of all the West's glacial lakes, is just a few miles away. The Kolbachs have also opened a business development center on the campus where, among other things, young people come to learn the basics of wind energy.

For information on the town and the retreat center, visit www .experiencegarysd.com or phone (605) 272-7777.

The plaza at Buffalo Ridge Resort

A Different Kind of Drive

Gary

Car-chase scenes replaced cattle drives in Hollywood when westerns lost their luster, but you can see the real thing in Gary, where the Klamrath family herds their cattle down Main Street every autumn. It usually happens on the last Saturday of October, but the exact date depends on "when the grass goes bad."

Twenty years ago the tradition almost halted because a few townspeople complained to the town board about stampeding cattle, terrified pedestrians, horses on lawns, and manure on the street. The ranchers denied any such ruckus.

The Gary newspaper editorialized that it preferred cattle on the road to some humans. "The cattle are more predictable and don't drive 3,000-pound hunks of wheeled steel around at high speed while under the influence of alcohol," wrote the editor.

After a war of words in the paper, the town board voted to allow cattle drives if the cowboys applied for a special permit and cleaned up after the cows.

You may encounter other cattle drives on South Dakota's rural roads, as ranchers move their herds from summer grazing pastures to winter quarters. But only in Gary can you watch the excitement from downtown. When the cattle leave, the townspeople gather for a soup lunch and crafts sale.

Cottonwood with Nine Lives

Henry

The luckiest tree in South Dakota towers over the little main street of Henry. Planted when the town was founded in 1882, the cottonwood has survived several fires and numerous storms.

In recent years it lived through a 1971 tornado that trimmed 10 feet off its top (it's still 85 feet high), another big windstorm in 1984, and a major fire that destroyed the Big Tree Cafe and Bar but left the

★ ★

big tree standing. Of course, it was spared when 500 other old trees were demolished as part of the Spruce Up South Dakota program.

Is the town as tough as the tree? It seems so. After losing population for many years, Henry (population 300) is also starting to grow.

Spurs and Saddles
Hitchcock

Where in the West can you find a hundred pairs of spurs, century-old saddles, and horsehair bridles made by prisoners? Your best bet is the Hitchcock Museum, a store full of collectibles amassed over a forty-year period by Ray and Rita Waldner.

There are stories behind the museum pieces, and the Waldners are happy to tell them. One of the fanciest sets of spurs belonged to singer Bob Wills of the Texas Playboys. South Dakota singer/songwriter Kyle Evans rode in one of the saddles. Another saddle was made by the Hamley saddle company of nearby Ashton in 1883. The company still makes saddles in Oregon.

The Waldners also have leather art by Bob Brown, whom Norman Rockwell once called "The Leonardo of Leather." Other oddities include $5 bills signed by celebrities, a license plate collection, and Hitchcock's original jail. Call (605) 266-2769 for an appointment to

Trivia

Hitchcock is the town to mix a museum visit with a meal. Just down the street, the DK Cafe (605-266-2181) serves country cooking seven days a week from 6:30 a.m. to 10:00 p.m.—and the small kitchen crew still finds time to prepare a locally famous Sunday smorgasbord.

see the museum, which is located in a 1908 auto dealer's showroom (372 Clark Street).

Cathedral of the Prairie
Hoven

Majestic cathedrals can be toured in Rome or Paris or, if you're traveling past the corn and wheat fields of north-central South Dakota, in Hoven (population 511).

The Cathedral of the Prairie at Hoven

★ ★

The grand St. Anthony's Catholic Church of Hoven (524 Main Street) doesn't quite qualify as a cathedral because no bishop resides in the little farming town. Still, Dakotans immediately dubbed it the Cathedral of the Prairie, and it seems a sin to argue the title on such a technicality.

Father Anthony Helmbrecht came to Hoven from Bavaria, Germany, in 1908 and soon persuaded his pioneer flock that a great cathedral—like those he'd known in Europe—could be built. So the men in town dug a 64-by-161-foot foundation and began construction. They were still at ground level ten years later, but in 1921 the Catholics of Hoven celebrated Easter in one of the finest houses of worship on the Northern Plains.

No expense was spared. Twin steeples rise 130 feet in the air. Twelve tall Bavarian-painted windows illustrate the life of Christ. Three two-ton bells ring from the spires, and the north tower has a huge clock that still keeps perfect time.

Sixty long oak pews seat more than a thousand people—so there's plenty of room at 7:00 a.m. daily masses (plus 5:00 p.m. Saturday and 10:00 a.m. Sunday). A bishop would be especially welcome.

Call the rectory at (605) 948-2451 to schedule a tour.

Hubert Humphrey Country

Huron

South Dakota is rock-ribbed Republican, but Hubert H. Humphrey is fondly remembered in Huron. In fact, his father's Humphrey Drug Store is still open for business on the main street—physical testimony to the fact that while Democrats are seldom allowed to hold high elected office within the state of South Dakota, they are welcome to engage in capitalism and the other privileges of a democracy.

Humphrey grew up in nearby Doland and worked at the pharmacy from 1933 to 1937; then he departed for Minnesota and a long political career. He served as a U.S. senator from Minnesota and as

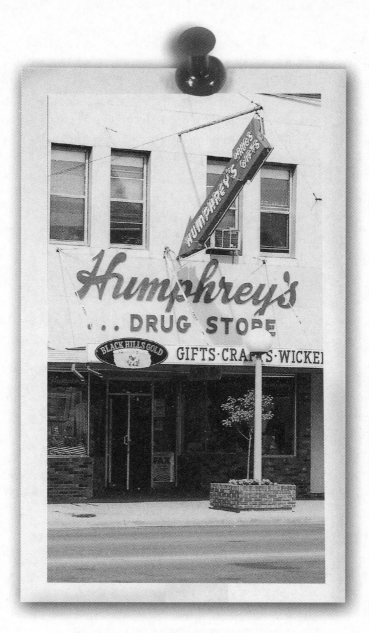

Hubert Humphrey's family pharmacy in Huron
SOUTH DAKOTA MAGAZINE

vice president under Lyndon Johnson in the 1960s. Richard Nixon defeated him in the 1968 presidential contest.

Humphrey's Drug Store has campaign materials and pictures from the famous native son's career. More HHH memorabilia can be seen at the Old Stone Church (aka the Centennial Center), a native stone structure just blocks away from the drugstore that serves as a history center and gathering place.

The drugstore—now owned by Ralph Gosch, a nephew of the ebullient politician—is at 233 Dakota Avenue South, Huron's main thoroughfare. The phone number is (605) 352-4064.

A Really Good Fair Singer
Huron

Sherwin Linton is better than a fair singer—stalwart country music fans have known that for years. But what else do you call a guy who has performed for more than thirty years (and counting) at the South Dakota State Fair in Huron, as well as other fairs throughout the country?

Linton generally plays three times a day at the fair, which is South Dakota's annual celebration of summer's end. Fans sit under giant shade trees near the outdoor Centennial Stage and listen to Linton, wife Pam, and their veteran band.

The Volga native (and Watertown High School alum) made his first guitar from a cigar box and yardstick. As a young man he journeyed to Nashville in the 1960s and gained attention with his big hit, "The Cotton King."

Today Linton is a country music legend. He always had talent, but now his longevity really hits a chord. Linton plays up to 250 dates a year. He's been entertaining for more than fifty years, and he has never missed a performance. That feat landed him in the _Guinness Book of World Records_. For more information on Linton, and his show schedule, visit www.sherwinlinton.com.

Singer Sherwin Linton
SHERWIN LINTON

★ ★

Whatchamacallit River

James River

If the James River had gained a foot of water every time its name was changed, it might be a friendlier waterway for boaters. Dakota tribes called it *E-ta-zi-po-ka-se*, meaning "unnavigable river." French explorers called it the *Riviere aux Jacques*. The U.S. Congress officially named it the Dakota River, but nobody paid attention to those guys in Washington.

The Frenchmen's name stuck, but settlers simplified it to the James, and befitting American slang, it has even been shortened to the Jim.

Though its name keeps changing, the river is as flat and crooked as ever. In some stretches it only drops a few inches in elevation per mile. The online encyclopedia Wikipedia declares it the longest unnavigable river in the entire world. That's because the shallow river wiggles and curves for 710 miles, starting in North Dakota and winding its way across East River until emptying into the Missouri just a few miles east of Yankton.

So enjoy the James, or Jim, or Jacques, or whatever—but don't bother bringing your 40-foot yacht.

Trivia

While at the state fair, stand in line for the famous BBQ rib sandwich from the South Dakota Pork Producers' food booth, watch the horse-pull competition, see 4–Hers grooming their thousand-pound steers—then you're on your own. For advance information call the fair at (800) 529-0900 or visit www.sdstatefair.com.

★ ★

The Man Behind the Lake
Lake Cochrane

A man can't really found a lake, but if anyone could, it was B. J. Cochrane, the first white settler in Deuel County. He arrived in 1872, built a home by the lake that now honors his name, and plowed the prairie sod with oxen.

B. J. Cochrane's farmhouse still stands by Lake Cochrane.
SOUTH DAKOTA MAGAZINE

★ ★

Cochrane was a much-loved lake character. Then, at age eighty-one, a serious hernia threatened his life, and the family was gathered. The doctor said he could operate, but the chances of survival were one in a hundred. Everyone fell quiet. Then the old man of the lake said, "Well, doc, load me in your wagon, take me down, and kill me scientifically."

So the doctor operated and Cochrane died—eighteen years later—at the age of ninety-nine years, ten months, and four days. Cochranes still live on the shore of Lake Cochrane, which is one of several lakes in South Dakota's Glacial Lakes region that remain crystal clear and virtually free of pollution.

Don't Eat the Leaves at Leola
Leola

Bitterness grows from a good thing used in excess, and that's especially true of rhubarb. Did you know its leaves are poisonous, for example? That you shouldn't eat the stalks in months with an *r* in their spelling? And that it can induce vomiting?

Such wisdom is bandied about at the Rhubarb Festival, held during odd-numbered years in the very German city of Leola, which touts itself as the Rhubarb Capital of the World. Rhubarb royalty are crowned, and the citizens also host a parade, a rhubarb goodies contest, turtle races, bed races, a street fair, and possibly a presentation by the author of the best-selling book *The Joy of Rhubarb.*

Awards are also bestowed for biggest leaf, biggest stalk, and tallest rhubarb structure. Call (605) 439-3109 or 439-3454 for particulars or the next date.

Fighting the Devil at Prairie Village
Madison

Did the devil stow away on the trains, covered wagons, steamboats, and stagecoaches that brought the settlers westward? He got here

Buffalo, Badgers, and Birds

Even if you miss the Rhubarb Festival, you'll still want to experience the grassland wilderness called Ordway Prairie, just 10 miles west of Leola. The 7,800-acre preserve is rich with wildlife, from buffalo to badgers to birds, and has more than 300 plant species and 400 wetlands (this is called the Prairie Pothole region). Be sure to take drinking water and binoculars. Call (605) 439-3475 for more information.

A baby bison frolicking on the prairie
SOUTH DAKOTA TOURISM

★ ★

some way or another, so it was necessary to quickly build churches and do battle.

Towns were starting and failing all over the prairie, so how was a missionary pastor to know where to build his church? A few wise preachers hit on the idea of a church on wheels, a chapel car that would travel with the railroad. Baptists, Episcopalians, and Catholics all tried chapel cars. When the train pulled into a tiny prairie hamlet, it wasn't unusual to see every man, woman, and child in town climb aboard and squeeze into the pews.

Eventually churches were built, and the pastors no longer had to chase up and down the iron tracks. But the chapel cars played an important role in fighting the devil on the frontier.

Only a handful of the cars still exist. One can be seen at the huge Prairie Village Museum, which lies on the outskirts of Madison by

Prairie Village celebrates Railroad Days every June.
SOUTH DAKOTA MAGAZINE

Lake Herman. Called the Emmanuel Car, it is still outfitted with pews, an old organ, and huge wooden GOD IS LOVE letters over glass.

Prairie Village, with streets full of very old buildings and furnishings, has something for everyone. Kids love the antique wood carousel, and grandparents relive the past in a town that looks a century old. Major festivals include Railroad Days in June and a threshing jamboree in late August. Call (800) 693-3655 for dates and details.

Lawrence Welk Was Here
Mansfield

We want our hometowns to be famous, and there's no easier way to accomplish that than by association. Maybe Custer camped in your town, or Jesse James stole your great-granddaddy's horses. Perhaps Teddy Roosevelt hunted in your hills, or John Dillinger robbed your bank.

Proudly, all that and more happened in South Dakota. Only a few towns can lay claim to a Custer or Dillinger story, but almost every community in the state has a barn, dance hall, or public auditorium where Lawrence Welk once played.

Younger readers may need to be told that Welk was the king of polka, the master of the accordion, and host of television's wildly popular *Lawrence Welk Show*. He grew up just north of South

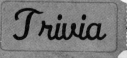

Trivia

Lawrence Welk's longtime sidekick, accordionist Myron Floren, grew up east of Aberdeen in a little town called Roslyn. He got his start when he became "The Melody Man" on KSOO Radio in Sioux Falls.

★ ★

Dakota (yes, that would be North Dakota). It was a familiar story: His father wanted him to be a farmer; Lawrence wanted to be a rock star, or the 1920s equivalent. Lawrence struck a deal: If his dad would buy him an accordion, he'd work on the farm until he was twenty-one before leaving for riches and fame.

Welk left on his twenty-first birthday for Aberdeen, then Watertown, then Yankton—playing wherever he and his band were welcomed. His Honolulu Fruit Gum Orchestra performed live on

Certainly, Lawrence Welk played his accordion here.

Yankton's big radio station, WNAX 570 AM, in the late 1920s, spreading Welk's name across the Midwest. By 1951 he hit Los Angeles, and the rest is champagne-music history.

There's nary a town or barn in East River, South Dakota, where someone doesn't claim to have heard Lawrence Welk play—and that includes a few buildings constructed after he departed the state. But we're certain he played in Mansfield, a cute little town just south of Aberdeen, because a big sign on the old town hall says so.

Two Coincidences Too Many
Marvin

How did Benedictine monks end up on a farm near the tiny town of Marvin in northeast South Dakota? There's a curious story to the founding of Blue Cloud Abbey.

The monks of St. Meinrad Abbey in Indiana wanted to establish a new monastery in the Dakotas, so they sent four brothers to scout the territory in 1949. They liked a spot above the Missouri River near Yankton, but WNAX Radio's tall towers obstructed the view. After failing to find what they wanted in South Dakota, they decided to drive to Fargo, North Dakota. On the way they stopped outside Marvin and saw the rolling, wooded hills above Grant County's Whetstone Valley.

Even though the land was rocky, they liked it, so they went to nearby Milbank to inquire. They were sent to see a Milbank banker, who told them that the land had just been listed for sale within the last thirty minutes. He offered them 300 acres at $22 an acre.

Their good timing and the banker's name were signs they couldn't ignore, so the Benedictine monks immediately inked the deal. The banker's name? Effner Benedict.

Two dozen monks now work and pray at Blue Cloud, which is located west of Milbank near US 12. Visitors are welcome, and the monks occasionally conduct retreats for laypeople. Information can be found at the monastery's Web site, www.bluecloud.org.

Monks work and pray at Blue Cloud Abbey.
SOUTH DAKOTA MAGAZINE

Saltwater Lake on the Prairie

Medicine Lake

Waterfowl frequent most of northeast South Dakota's Glacial Lakes, but not Medicine Lake, north of Henry in Codington County. If a duck or goose inadvertently lands there, it will take flight immediately. Fish can't survive in the water, but humans cannot sink in it because of the high mineral content. It was once a popular resort lake because swimmers enjoyed the buoyancy and some thought the water had healing qualities.

Why is Medicine Lake so different from neighboring bodies of water? Geologists believe it's because a large mineral water spring feeds the lake on its west side. The water is often so clear that you can read a book through it from a dozen feet away—if you can read wet pages from a dozen feet . . . the water won't cure nearsightedness.

Menno's Sense of Humus

Menno

Farmer-writer E. B. White once noted, "A good farmer is nothing more or less than a handy man with a sense of humus." Nowhere is that better displayed than at the annual Menno Power Show, held the third weekend of September.

When seen from a distance of twenty-five to thirty years, troublesome tractors (and aren't they all?) that once tested the patience and language of Dakota farmers take on a glamorous sheen that blinds the victims to sufferings once endured.

Proof of that can be found at Menno and at other farm equipment and threshing exhibitions every autumn. At Menno the tractors parade around a large collection of old barns, depots, churches, and other historic buildings that have been moved to the exhibition site on the north side of town. Old-style foods, music, demonstrations,

★ ★

and exhibits provide diverse entertainment. Visit www.mennosd.org for additional information on Menno and its Power Show.

"Ah, well; there is no harm done in looking back wistfully at this distance," wrote Dakota Territory author Hamlin Garland. "At this distance it is safe enough."

Farm nostalgia draws crowds to Menno's Power Show.
SOUTH DAKOTA MAGAZINE

Mining the Hard Stuff

Milbank

Some of the universe's hardest and oldest rocks are mined near Milbank. The deposits of Dakota granite are thought to be four billion years old. You'd have to go to the moon to find an older kitchen countertop . . . and think of the weight you'd be adding on the return flight. So Milbank is your best bet. Customers arrive from around the world, drawn by the stone's high quartz content, which accounts for both the hardness and its rich, light red color.

Native Americans made pipes and utensils from a soft version of quartzite that came to be called pipestone. Pioneer town-builders used the stone for cemetery headstones, for foundations, and even for entire structures. The towns of Dell Rapids, Flandreau, and Milbank, along with downtown Sioux Falls, are especially blessed with granite architecture.

The economic value of the rock increased dramatically when synthetic, diamond-tipped saw blades became available. Several quarries operate in the Milbank area, including the Stengel family's Dakota Granite, founded in 1925. More than 200 truckloads from the Cold Spring Granite Company were sent to Washington, D.C., in the 1990s for construction of the Franklin Delano Roosevelt Memorial.

Trivia

If you visit Menno on a Tuesday, dine at Rita Hoff's main street cafe, The Open Door, because that's German Day. You'll be treated to delights like knepflad, schlactplatte, hackbraten, maultaschen, sauerbraten, or others that you may not be able to pronounce . . . because you'll have your mouth full.

South Dakota's four borders were marked with granite posts more than a century ago. A marker was erected every mile, but many have since been lost to soil erosion or thieves. Some resourceful South Dakota farmers have tried using granite as fence posts. They last longer than cedar or pine, but it takes some muscle to nail the barbed wire.

Grist for Travelers
Milbank

A UFO would barely seem more out of place along US 12 in Milbank than Henry Holland's 1882 windmill.

Holland, an English settler, built a 44-foot-high wood structure to mill wheat for Grant County farmers in the nineteenth century. However, Milbank's growing trees and houses soon blocked the wind from turning the 30-foot vanes. The mill, though beautifully constructed, was soon abandoned.

In 1912 history-minded citizens bought the gristmill and moved it to the city park. Needing preservation again in 1978, the Holland mill was given to Milbank Mutual. The insurance company moved it

Batterrrrup!

Baseball fans will want to seek out the granite monument near the ball field at the east end of town that memorializes Milbank as the birthplace of American Legion baseball. The nationwide program was started here in July 1925 by WWI veterans who thought boys were losing interest in the all-American game. Now more than 90,000 teens grab a glove every summer.

to their office grounds, where up until recently it stood as the town's welcoming symbol, doubling as a visitor center in the summer. Townspeople embarked on a multiyear project to restore the original, but they kept replacing the boards. The final result was a new mill that looks like Henry's and grinds grain as well or better. Old or new, it is still the town's favorite symbol.

Old or new, it still grinds grain.

★ ★

A Stickler for Gray
Mitchell

Oscar Howe ranks as one of America's great artists, but at the age of twenty-five he was just another struggling artist, so in 1940 he was more than pleased to do a mural in the dome of the Carnegie Library in downtown Mitchell for $65. The money came from a Depression-

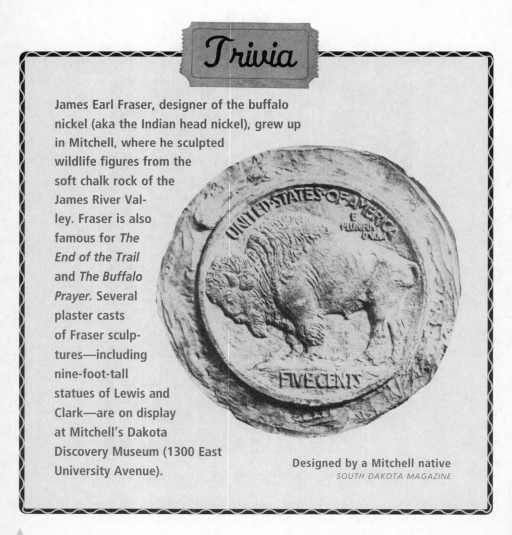

Trivia

James Earl Fraser, designer of the buffalo nickel (aka the Indian head nickel), grew up in Mitchell, where he sculpted wildlife figures from the soft chalk rock of the James River Valley. Fraser is also famous for *The End of the Trail* and *The Buffalo Prayer*. Several plaster casts of Fraser sculptures—including nine-foot-tall statues of Lewis and Clark—are on display at Mitchell's Dakota Discovery Museum (1300 East University Avenue).

Designed by a Mitchell native
SOUTH DAKOTA MAGAZINE

era New Deal program designed to employ out-of-work artists and writers.

Howe incorporated his Sioux culture's spiritual Four Directions, which use the colors black, red, yellow, and white to represent man's connection to his environment. He also had a two-dimensional style, a carryover from when his ancestors painted on animal skins.

About three decades later, historians and art enthusiasts in Mitchell happily received a grant to restore the mural, and they were delighted to learn that Howe—who had since achieved greatness—might visit their project. As the restorers were completing their work, Howe walked into the entrance, took one look at his very first mural, and asked, "Where are the gray lines?"

Mitchell's Carnegie Library, home to a mural by Lakota artist Oscar Howe.

★ ★

"What gray lines?" asked the workers. It's lucky he stopped by. Howe showed the young restorers how he had bordered the dome with faint gray lines to create the effect of a skin painting, but the gray had since faded. Today the staff will figure you are either a smarty-pants or a savvy art historian if you visit the Carnegie Resource Center at 119 West Third Avenue and ask, "Where are the gray lines?"

The center serves as a small museum and history research center for the region. The volunteer staff considers it their duty to preserve the mural, gray lines and all.

The Truth Behind the Corn Palace
Mitchell

Mitchell's children grow up thinking every town has a Corn Palace. Some probably reach grade school before wondering why strangers with funny-looking license plates are parking by their basketball gym. By the time they hit puberty, they start to overhear those visitors referring to the Corn Palace as schmaltzy. Then, as the kids enter their teen years, they become very confused about the real purpose of their town's landmark.

Of course, adversity is a character builder, and as a group experience, it creates lifelong bonds and friendships, so the Corn Palace is really not about getting travelers off the highway. It's a way to raise strong and confident youths.

That's as schmaltzy as the Corn Palace, but it's not entirely false. Mitchell built the Corn Palace (603 North Main Street) in 1892 to promote pride in South Dakota's agricultural promise. Corn had been around for about 9,000 years, so it didn't need publicity, and there was no highway, so tourism wasn't even a dream. Mitchell just wanted to advertise that we could grow corn and wheat like the best of them. The town's leaders never imagined they would one day sell T-shirts and coffee mugs on the basketball floor all summer long.

The town's citizenry takes the Corn Palace seriously. They

The Corn Palace is the best friend Kodak ever had.
SOUTH DAKOTA TOURISM

redecorate every year with colored corn grown specifically for the designs, which are created by fine artists. Even the famous Lakota artist Oscar Howe once designed the huge outdoor panels. This is art, history, kitsch, capitalism, and child development all rolled into one big palace. And did we mention that we can really raise corn?

A good time to visit is late summer during the Corn Palace Festival, featuring a rodeo and big-name entertainers. Call (605) 996-5031 for more information on the museum or the festival.

Can You Hear Corn Grow?

While traveling East River in mid-summer, you'll see countless fields of corn—the dark green, thick-leafed plant that sprouts a foot-long ear in August and turns golden brown in September. Biologically, it's classified as a grass.

Many farmers insist you can hear corn grow if you spend some quiet time in a field on a hot, still summer's night. And why not? Corn goes from a kernel to 7 feet in about a hundred days. What wouldn't crackle and pop at that rate?

Interestingly, the best watermelons grow in the shade of tall corn. If you're caught in a watermelon patch after dark, however, and it's not your patch, the only believable excuse will be to say, "I'm on my way over to listen to the corn . . . "

Best listening months are July and August.
JOHN FRONT

A Welder Says a Thousand Words

Montrose

Wayne Porter says he can't draw, paint, or carve. But vultures, dragons, and other magical beasts take shape when he gathers scrap metal around his welder. Just as the painter dips his brush in his soul, so Porter does with his welding rods. His creations are more than mere figurines—they make you think and laugh.

He started Porter's Sculpture Park in a field along I-90 in 2000, and it has developed into a busy affair. Porter is there seven days a week in the summer months, greeting guests and working on new

Wayne Porter's huge sculptures are visible from I-90.
WAYNE PORTER

★ ★

pieces. That's ironic for a forty-something fellow who studied political science and history at South Dakota State University because he was concerned that art would be all consuming. He dabbled in various enterprises, including sheep ranching in Hand County, before entering the field of sculpture.

And it is a field, literally—ten acres of dragons, butterflies, vultures, and the like. There's a boy on a sled, and a man's head with a hand reaching out from the brain for ideas. The butterfly is landing on a giant finger, and the vultures are lined up like fence posts.

Everybody's favorite is the 60-foot-tall longhorn that's the same height as the heads on Mount Rushmore. Teddy Roosevelt would say "Bully!" And that's just the right spirit. Made of 8-inch-square steel plates from abandoned railroad tracks, the bull weighs twenty-five tons.

Porter's newest project is a 30-foot claw hammer pulling a huge nail from a concrete pad. He's looking for a giant crane to lift the hammer in place.

Porter's Sculpture Park is 25 miles west of Sioux Falls at the Montrose exit along I-90 (watch for the 60-foot bull). Call (605) 204-0370 for more information.

A Musician's Homecoming
Parkston

A taste of Los Angeles is exhibited on Parkston's main street, thanks to a human condition called "roots."

Ken Klauss grew up in Parkston, the son of a German immigrant blacksmith. Known as "Mr. Music" in high school, he graduated in 1940 and left for California to work in the defense industry during World War II. Klauss was gay, an agnostic, and hungry for a career in the music industry, so it wasn't a surprise that he felt comfortable there. After studying at the University of Southern California, he became a successful classical songwriter, musician, and choreographer. One of his scores, *Dedication to Jose Clemente Orozco,* is now in the Library of Congress.

The 1990s had highs and lows for Klauss. He was invited to Washington, D.C., to perform the Orozco music. His longtime partner, Bernard James, died. And in 1994, he bought an old, abandoned bank building at 100 West Main Street. His South Dakota roots were pulling him home.

Using $100,000 that James had left him and assistance from his sister, he spent about $300,000 to restore the two-story structure into what's now the Klauss Archives and James Art Museum. Klauss's career notes, writings, and tapes are stored in the bank vault. A

Reflections of the Klauss Archives
SOUTH DAKOTA MAGAZINE

★ ★

concert piano, family photos, and other memorabilia are exhibited on the main floor. And many of his partner's best paintings hang in a second-story gallery that also offers a picturesque view of the little city.

A board in Parkston helps Klauss oversee the museum, and he established an endowment so it will continue. He spends Aprils and Septembers there, giving tours and an occasional South Dakota performance. The blacksmith's son, who still speaks fluent German, enjoys talking about his boyhood days in Parkston. Soft-spoken yet talkative—with a brush of white hair and a blacksmith's modest grin—he hopes he doesn't come off as pompous to South Dakotans. "I try not to because those are the people that bug me!"

Visitors are welcome to tour the museum, whether Klauss is there or not. But he's as interesting as the paintings and photos, so try to visit in April or September. The museum is open Thursday through Saturday from 11:00 a.m. to 1:00 p.m. or call (605) 928–3833 for an appointment.

Decriminalizing Graffiti
Redfield

Like it or not, graffiti is one of America's newest art forms. They especially like it in Redfield, where high school seniors are invited to scribble on the spillway to Turtle Creek during homecoming week.

Turtle Creek flows through the middle of Redfield, but it hardly divides the community because the town has built parks, greenways, and a fine walking bridge crafted by local welders to keep everyone connected. At the far end of the creek, a spillway forms a small lake, where a public campground welcomes travelers.

Since 9/11 the students have been painting patriotic imagery on the concrete and signing their names. The youths wear safety harnesses hooked to a cable so they don't fall down the steep spillway.

Their red, white, and blue drawings give graffiti—and teenagers—a good name to all who cross Turtle Creek on US 212.

Legal graffiti on the Turtle Creek spillway

★ ★

A Store of Empty Bottles
Ree Heights

All food stores have shelves full of bottles, but not the variety you'll see at the Ree Heights Grocery, where most of them are empty and old.

Delton and Carol Beck have been running the store and adding to their bottle collection since 1978, when their son Jared first started to scavenge for interesting glass. He came home with bottles that had held milk, soda, liquor, perfumes, medicines, meats, cleaners, and an assortment of other liquids and solids. Once the collection was started, customers brought in unique bottles. Today the tiny store has 1,000 bottles—including many from foreign countries—and that doesn't include those shiny new ones with price tags that are still full of ketchup or barbecue sauce.

Ree Heights (population 70) is lucky to still have a grocery store, and even more fortunate to have one that draws international visitors. Signatures in the guest book show that people from all over the world enjoy the nostalgia and history represented in bottles.

Carol closes on Monday and Saturday afternoons, but if you drive past on US 14 and want to see the bottles, you're welcome to call (605-943-5532) and she'll reopen. The store is easy to find—Ree Heights' main street is one block long.

Trivia

You've heard of Ree Heights? Then you must be a fan of professional rodeo. The famous Etbauer brothers (Robert, Billy, and Danny), the saddle bronc family dynasty, grew up outside town. You'll find their family's brand, along with other cowboys' marks, on the bar at Shakey's, the town's saloon, at 118 Dakota Avenue.

Lotsa Llamas

While in Redfield, find the Two Bridges Llama Farm (a few miles northeast of town at 38755 170th Street), where Kathy Maddox knits and sells stylish ladies' caps, hats, and scarves made from the herd's wool. She wore out her right thumb from knitting, but a doctor replaced some of the bone and she started again. You're welcome to pet the llamas, but be ready to duck: They spit!

Llamas at Two Bridges

Named Twice

Salem, South Dakota, was named after the city of witches in Massachusetts only because the town's first postmaster hailed from there. However, the name was changed to Melas (Salem backwards) because a nearby town called itself Salena, and Salem's town fathers didn't like the similarity. When Salena died (apparently, no witchcraft was involved), they again reversed the spelling.

The Vinegar Man
Roslyn

It may leave a sour taste in your mouth, but don't let that stop you from visiting the world's only vinegar museum.

Lawrence Diggs, known as the Vinegar Man, is founder-in-chief of the International Vinegar Museum (104 West Carlton Avenue) in the tiny northern town of Roslyn, which until the museum opened was best known as accordionist Myron Floren's birthplace.

The town of 225 people opened its handsome old brick town hall to Diggs when he arrived from California with a dream to educate the world about the wonders of vinegar. He's doing a good job. Along with the museum he has founded an annual vinegar festival, published books, and traveled across the country and overseas to research and teach the uses of vinegar.

Did you know that vinegar kills bacteria, cleans windows, and makes piecrust flakier? Museum visitors learn all that and more, plus they get to taste vinegars from around the world. How do you taste vinegar? Breathe the aroma, then swirl it on your tongue. Everybody in Roslyn knows that.

★ ★

The museum is open June to Labor Day. A small admission fee is charged, but "instant scholarships" are awarded for anyone who finds it a hardship. Call (605) 486-4536 for more information.

Is a Coteau a Good Place for a Cabin?
Sisseton

Even some who live there can't define Coteau des Praires. Actually, those are just fancy French words for "hills of the prairie," and they refer specifically to the high country that forms a continental divide in the Glacial Lakes country of northeast South Dakota. Lake Traverse, on the north side of the hills, flows to the Red River Valley of North Dakota and then into Hudson Bay in Canada. To the south the

Climb the Nicollet Tower for a glacial view.

85

Coteau des Prairies is drained by the Big Sioux River, which flows to the Missouri and on to the Mississippi.

Twenty million years ago, huge ice glaciers bulldozed in a slow crawl across this country, shaping the hills and valleys. When the ice age ended, the melting water created the lakes and potholes that we now call the Glacial Lakes of northeast South Dakota.

French explorer Joseph Nicollet arrived in 1838 to find a paradise of hills, grasslands, wildlife, and water. In a journal entry he said he admired a view (above today's Sisseton) so much that he might someday return to build a cabin there. Who hasn't made similar comments in our travels? Of course, like most tourists and explorers, he never came back.

However, today's Coteau citizens also appreciate that view of Long Valley. So much so that they decided to build a 75-foot observation tower in the 1990s so visitors could learn about Nicollet and the Coteau des Prairies he loved so well. You'll find it on SD 10, just above Sisseton.

The Onion Forecaster

Sisseton

For long-range rain forecasting, buy six onions or befriend Joe Schuch of Sisseton. Schuch learned to predict the weather from an old Swiss farmer. Here's how it works:

Take six locally grown onions. Between 11:00 p.m. and midnight on Christmas Eve, cut the onions lengthwise (stem to root) so you can see the layers. Remove all but the outer shell, which will seem like a bowl. Line the twelve halves in a row, and label them January through December. Add three-quarters tablespoon of pickling salt to each bowl. Cover with a cloth. In the morning remove the cloth and record the amount of moisture in each onion bowl. If it's going to be a wet month, the salt will be damp. For a really wet month, the salt will be saturated. Some months, the salt will be so dry you can pour it back into the shaker. That's a drought.

Schuch, a retired county agent in Roberts County, often included his onion predictions in the column he wrote for the local newspaper. After a few successes friends and neighbors began to take note. Nowadays he carries the forecast in his wallet and shares it over coffee at Billy's in downtown Sisseton. When people talk about the weather, they turn to him and ask, "Joe, what do the onions say?"

Joe Schuch, the Onion Forecaster

Beware the Upslope

Warning! Be careful if you travel here in winter. Long Hollow, south of Sica Hollow, lies about 1,200 feet above the town of Sisseton. The elevation allows for scenic views, but in winter it creates a weather phenomenon known as an upslope. The sudden elevation difference causes a decrease in air pressure, and that in turn creates an increase in wind speed as air rushes to fill the void. Add cold temperatures and snow, and Long Hollow becomes a killer. Atop the hill on SD 10, three historic markers relate some tragedies that occurred there.

TWO BROTHERS

A grove of tall, stately pine trees two miles north of this marker whisper the tale of two Dakota Indian brothers, Clarence and Joseph Grey, who died in an early winter snowstorm in November 1958, while trapping along the coteau. Their bodies were found the following spring under snowdrifts in the evergreen trees.

Clarence Grey was born February 10, 1918, and Joseph Grey was born August 31, 1921. Their parents were Andrew and Lilly Grey. Having grown up near Grey Lake, the brothers were expert fishermen, hunters, and trappers, just as their Dakota relatives had been for centuries. Joseph was also a World War II veteran, having received the Purple Heart for serious battle injuries.

Friends and neighbors of the deceased brothers say that when the winter winds blow through the pine trees, they can hear the Grey brothers singing hymns in the Dakota language. Maybe it is a reminder to travelers to be prepared for treacherous blizzards in this area.

SPONSORED BY THE HERITAGE MUSEUM OF ROBERTS COUNTY
AND THE SOUTH DAKOTA DEPARTMENT OF TRANSPORTATION
1998

Memorials to Long Hollow tragedies

Evil or Beautiful or Both?

Sisseton

There is a complicated East River forest where blood sometimes runs in the coulees, ghostly sightings are numerous, and mysterious moans and groans are heard in dark valleys. We can't explain all that, but we can help with your pronunciation. Say *See-chee* Hollow. That'll win points with the local folks.

As to whether Sica Hollow is haunted, who can say? If you fear ghosts, stay out of the hollow when the sun goes down. However,

Sica Hollow is a favorite autumn haunt.
SOUTH DAKOTA TOURISM

scientists wonder if methane emissions in the artesian springs might appear ghostly. Iron deposits might turn the water red. And trapped air in the waterways could make funny sounds as it escapes.

According to Indian legend, the hollow was peaceful until a stranger named Hand taught the boys to kill. A medicine man asked the Great Spirit for a return to peaceful times, and he sent Thunderer to fight Hand. Thunderer delivered a heavy rain to the forest, and the evil Hand became trapped by vines. Rainwater filled his mouth, and Thunderer's talons ripped out his eyes. All were killed by the flood except Fawn, who escaped to the hilltops. The hollow was peaceful again, but mysterious sounds were heard forevermore.

Say it again: *See-chee*. Now you're ready to explore the forest. It's one of the best places in South Dakota to enjoy autumn foliage. To get there, go 11 miles west of Sisseton on SD 10 and then go north for 5 miles on SD 25. The park's phone number is (605) 448-5701.

How Do You Measure a Pheasant?
Tinkertown

Pound for pound, the biggest bird in the West roosts in tiny Tinkertown, 12 miles west of Watertown along US 212. Some South Dakota cities might actually have taller pheasants, but Tinkertown's rooster was made of concrete in 1950 by the Walters, proprietors of a country store that operated there.

Either as a political statement or simply because they thought the pheasant was lonely, the Walters added a concrete donkey known as Depression Nag. Girl Scouts from Clark have helped to paint the pair through the years.

South Dakota claims to be one of the first states to successfully import the Chinese ring-necked pheasant, so several communities have competed for the title of Pheasant Capital. Huron boasts the world's biggest pheasant (40 feet from beak to tail feather), but it's a plastic lightweight compared to Tinkertown's. Gregory and

Redfield—two other places rich in pheasant lore—also have big plastic birds along their main thoroughfares.

But the biggest (pound for pound) and oldest bird still stands in Tinkertown. Guy Fish runs a welding and repair shop there, and he says families still stop to pose their kids by the pheasant. Often the parents comment that they had their picture taken there in the 1950s. That's a long life for a ring-necked rooster in a state famous for pheasant hunting.

The Tinkertown pheasant

★ ★

Happy Birthday, St. John
Turton

St. John the Baptist's birthday is remembered every June on the weekend closest to the saint's feast day, the 24th, by the town of Turton (population 60). Parishioners and guests celebrate with a mass at historic St. Joseph's Catholic Church, a golf tournament, softball, street dance, and special foods.

The tradition dates to 1899, making it one of South Dakota's oldest continual celebrations and one of the nation's oldest birthday parties for any saint other than St. Patrick and St. Nick.

St. John's birthday is celebrated at St. Joe's.
KATIE HUNHOFF

92

Vienna's Coffee Tradition

Vienna

Immigrants from Vienna, Austria, settled the tiny town of Vienna in Clark County. The Austrian original (population 1.6 million) has a reputation for lively coffeehouses, where people gather to socialize. South Dakota's Vienna (pronounced *VY-anna,* by the way) also has a coffee tradition.

Since there's no restaurant in the town of seventy-eight people, postmistress Myra Cluts brings coffee and home-baked treats to work so people have a place to gather both mornings and afternoons. Not a bad place to buy your stamps.

Vienna: where stamps come with coffee

★ ★

Don't Eat Soup at the Turtle Races
Volin

Can a mud turtle crawl faster than a painted, or should we go for size with a snapper? Turtle racers must make such choices—and there are more. Do you feed your turtle on race morning? What do you feed it? Does it help to cheer? Will a snapper really bite your finger off?

The first Volin Turtle Races in the 1970s were a big hit, but the frivolity soured when it was learned that the young entrepreneurs who organized the event were selling turtle soup before the sun went down. A few years ago, the races were resurrected without soup sales; now the hard-shellers get all the respect an athlete deserves.

The rules are simple. Bring your turtle and put him under the barrel on Main Street with all the rest. When the barrel is lifted, the turtles crawl for the finish line . . . and crawl . . . and crawl. This isn't for the speedy NASCAR crowd; it's a quiet way to spend a summer day, and the kids and turtles all go home happy.

The Volin Turtle Races are held on a Saturday in June. Call Corey Logan at (605) 660-6006 for details.

Here's a tip: Snapping turtles usually don't race well. They are surly and slow, and even when they do win, they are sticks-in-the-mud at post-race parties. Put your money on the painted turtles.

A Popular Outlaw
Wagner

Nails from the coffin of Jack Sully are on exhibit at the Charles Mix County Museum in Wagner, along with a deck of cards that belonged to the Irishman who became a local legend. Why such affection for an outlaw? Even today, local historians debate whether Sully was a rustler or a martyr.

Sully began his life in Dakota Territory as an establishment lawman. He was part of a mob that lynched two rustlers. Later, many wondered whether the roles somehow got reversed that day, but Sully used the opportunity to run for sheriff. He won 61–1, impressive when you realize there were only fifty-five eligible voters.

In 1886 Sully sold timber rights on a Missouri River island to some men who quickly set to work harvesting the lumber. He failed to inform them, however, that it was actually Indian reservation land and he had no title to it. That omission nearly led to war, but to Sully's credit he accepted the blame.

He did many charitable acts: paying grocery tabs for poor families, helping struggling homesteaders with their work, and raising his eight children with love and attention. All the while he also organized a massive rustling ring that involved 300 men and continued for thirty years. Sully generally only stole a few cattle at a time. Ranchers figured if they complained, he might take more next time.

Efforts were made to nab Sully. He escaped one posse by hiding in a snowbank; on another occasion he dressed in the garb of an Indian woman and greeted lawmen as they passed his wagon.

In 1902 Sully was caught red-handed, branding a stolen calf. He escaped to Canada, but by 1904 South Dakota ranchers noticed their herds were shrinking, and they figured that he had returned. A posse chased him through the Rosebud country. Shots were exchanged; Sully's horse stumbled, and the rustler fell to the ground with at least five bullet wounds. He shook the marshal's hand before he died.

We suspect you're wondering why the coffin nails are aboveground. We wonder, too. Did he escape once again?

To see the nails and other novelties, visit the museum located on East SD 50 in Wagner. Call (605) 384-5212 for museum hours.

A Senatorial Pumpkin Man
Watertown

As a state legislator, Don Brosz was serious about taxation, education, and regulation. He dressed in dark suits and spoke with an authoritative voice—until the pumpkins on his small farm would turn orange. Then, Senator Brosz donned an orange suit and a big smile and invited everyone to his Pumpkin Patch.

★ ★

Brosz no longer has to wear two hats. He has retired from politics, and now he's known by young and old as just the Pumpkin Man. He began the tradition in 1991, and it won't be easy to stop. Hundreds of children and adults (sometimes by the busload) plan autumn pilgrimages to his Pumpkin Patch west of Watertown at 2530 Sioux Conifer Road. A pumpkin wagon provides rides around the three-acre garden, which is decorated for Halloween. Brosz charges just $2 per pumpkin. Some years he has sold more than 4,000, along with gourds and squash.

Call (605) 886-6237 for more information on the Pumpkin Patch.

Don Brosz (seated), with fellow Pumpkineers
DON BROSZ

Mixing Bagpipes and Brew
Watertown

Bill Dempsey was a sandwich salesman who was pretty good with the bagpipes, and so, very unlike the sad character in the famous play *Death of a Salesman,* Dempsey quit the road and bravely started his own brewpub in downtown Watertown.

Between brewing beer and serving customers, he'll sometimes don his red plaid kilt and play a mournful tune on the 'pipes. The music is excellent. In fact, the brewmeister is pipe major for the Glacial Lakes Pipe and Drum Corps.

Bill Dempsey (center) with the Glacial Lakes Pipe and Drum Corps

And how good is the beer? Well, of course, it depends on your taste buds: Dempsey brews Battle Axe Blond (a wheat beer), Valkyrie Red, Black Bear Stout, and Banshi Pale Ale. He maintains that light beer is a trick of the big beer companies to profit from water sales. If a patron asks for a light beer, Dempsey serves one of his regular beers with a glass of water on the side. "Make it as light as you want," he says.

Dempsey's Brewery, Pub & Restaurant (127 North Broadway) is in uptown Watertown, near the railroad tracks. Call (605) 882-9760 or visit www.dempseysbrewpub.com.

The Cane Capital
Watertown

Camaraderie exists among South Dakotans when it comes to walking canes. It's nothing organized, and hardly identifiable, but it exists. You might even say that a secret cane society has formed. On about the very day that any man or woman needs a cane, one usually appears—thanks to the generosity of a friend, relative, or perfect stranger. Oh, some people still go to the store to buy a cane, but they wouldn't have to if they just made their need known.

South Dakota has no specified headquarters for the society, but its spirit was possibly born in Watertown in 1979 after Melvin Hanthorn was in a truck accident and needed a cane. He made a diamond willow (the Cadillac of canes), and when he regained his footing, he gave it away to a friend who needed it. Then Mel made another cane, and another, and another.

He made 3,220 canes in all and gave them all away. A few friends joined in the good work of Uncle Mel's Cane Factory in later years, using their saws and lathes and carving knifes in Mel's garage on Seventh Street. Sticks of wood were kept in all four corners—walnut, hickory, cedar, and other varieties. Mel's favorite method was to glue three woods together and then use a wood lathe to create a pleasing spiral.

He'd spend up to three days hand-carving a diamond willow, plus time searching the river valley for suitable willow branches. The diamond design in the willow was created by nature: A fungus on the willow causes diamond-shaped cankers to grow.

Mel has had to close the factory for health reasons, but his canes will be walking the streets of the West for many years to come.

America's First Movie Is Missing

Watertown

Did Watertown's John Banvard create the first moving picture, or just a darned long painting? We'll let you decide.

Banvard was among the nineteenth century's most successful artists. Determined to create the largest painting in the world, he floated down the Mississippi in 1840 and sketched scenery. He went weeks without seeing another human being; then he retreated to a Louisville, Kentucky, warehouse to paint. He was separated from his family for fifteen years. The finished canvas was 12 feet high and stretched 3 miles.

Banvard invented a system of cylinders to wind the canvas and keep it from sagging or wearing. Then he took *Mississippi Panorama* on the road, narrating a story as the canvas was rolled across the stage. The scenery was so realistic that on one occasion a Street Louis businessman jumped up during the performance and shouted, "That's my store! Halloa there, captain! Stop the boat—I want to go ashore and see my wife and family!" He admitted later that he felt for an instant as if he were sailing the river in St. Louis.

Sadly, Banvard's business skills were not equal to his passion for painting. He fell into financial ruin, so he rolled up his famous painting and went to live in Watertown with his son, Eugene. He wrote one of South Dakota's first books, became active in politics, and even painted another panorama, a Civil War scene titled *The Burning of the Columbia.*

Today critics say Banvard's talent was in theater and showmanship rather than painting, but everyone would like to know what became of the 3-mile painting. One of Banvard's grandchildren remembers playing on it as a child. Some old-timers think part of the canvas was used as scenery in the Watertown Opera House. Others think it was shredded for home insulation. Or could it still be in some attic with a tall ceiling? Keep an eye on the rummage sales.

Serious Clowning
Watertown

Since the pharaohs of Egypt, almost every culture has had clowns. Don and Dorothy Crouse, along with family and friends, fill the bill in the lake country surrounding Watertown.

The Crouses were running a drugstore at Willow Lake in 1957 when the town celebrated its seventy-fifth birthday, so they rebuilt a Model T for the parade. Friends brought parts. The cab came from Elsena Busse's pasture, riddled with bullet holes. Henry Deters had a '25 chassis, and Art Kannegieter found a universal joint. So it went.

"We wanted something that would make people laugh, so we bolted a post on the back with a saddle," recalls Don. "Then we had the wheels welded off center so it would bounce up and down as it went down the street." One of his male friends dressed as a woman. (Laughs come easier in South Dakota than in the pharaoh's court.)

The car was a smash, and the Crouses have been clowning around at local parades and celebrations ever since. Their four children all joined the act, and now the grandkids are painting their faces and getting laughs. Friends and neighbors have also joined in.

Happiness and sadness are emotions equated with both love and clowns. "The clown is in essence a creature of love," wrote Beryl Hugill in her book *Bring on the Clowns.* That's quite obvious when you see Crouse and Crew parading down Main Street.

The Crouse clowns, funning around

Step into a Redlin

Watertown

Volunteers and staff at Watertown's Redlin Art Center (1200 Mickelson Drive) grew weary of hearing visitors say, "Oh, I wish I could just step inside that painting!" So they figured out a way, and built a life-size version of the log cabin from Terry Redlin's popular *Comforts of Home*.

Redlin, who has been named America's Most Popular Artist on several occasions, grew up in Watertown. After he lost a leg in a

★ ★

The home of artist Terry Redlin's original oils
SOUTH DAKOTA TOURISM

motorcycle accident, his home state funded his way to art school in
St. Paul. He later gained fame and fortune in Minnesota but came
back in the 1990s and built a $10 million art center, designed by his
son Charles, as payback.

Admission is free; overhead is funded by a gift shop and office
rentals on the top floor. More than 150 of Redlin's originals hang
in the gallery, along with dozens of prints. As you peruse the paintings, try to find the nine that include a Langenfeld Ice Cream sign.
Langenfeld's was a local dairy with a big following when the artist

was a boy. Not only did he like the ice cream, but he also married Helene Langenfeld. A collection of Langenfeld memorabilia, including ice-cream scoops and advertising items, are on display at the center, donated by local attorney Bob Wagner, whose father was chief ice-cream maker at the company.

Call (605) 882-3877 for more information on the center, or visit www.redlinart.com.

Imelda Would Love It
Webster

When Imelda Marcos, first lady of the Philippines, was ridiculed for her huge shoe collection, she retorted, "I do not have three thousand pair of shoes; I have one thousand and sixty!"

Imelda would be rather jealous of Mildred Fiksdal O'Neill's collection of 10,000 pairs. The difference between the two ladies is this: Mrs. Marcos bought shoes for herself and hid them away. Mrs. O'Neill has been collecting other people's shoes since she was a girl in the 1940s, and she shares them with the world at the Museum of Wildlife, Science and Industry located on West SD 12 in Webster.

Mrs. O'Neill, who was raised in Webster, returned to live in her hometown in 1994 and built a shoelike house on the museum grounds to display the collection. There are snowshoes, ice skates, cowboy boots, moccasins, Russian ballet slippers, safari shoes, and other unique pairs. Mrs. O'Neill is especially intrigued by a tiny replica of a leather boot that her late husband brought back from the Battle of the Bulge. "He heard some groaning on the battlefield, and it turned out to be a Nazi soldier," she explained. "My husband tended to him as well as he could, and as the German lay dying, he pulled out the little boot and gave it to him. He said it was his family's good luck charm. And then he died."

The museum is open daily except Monday from April through September. If you're lucky, Mrs. O'Neill might be volunteering on the day you stop. Call (605) 345-4751 for more information.

★ ★

A Crumpet with Your Tea?

Wessington Springs

Travelers are spoiled these days. Can you imagine someone asking where on the American prairie they might have an English tea in a thatched-roof cottage and, if you don't mind, perhaps a stroll in a Shakespearean garden?

Well, we do have such a place, old chap. Try the Anne Hathaway Cottage in Wessington Springs.

It began when Emma Shay, an English professor at Wessington Springs Seminary, traveled to England to study. While there she

A Shakespearean garden blooms near the cottage.
SOUTH DAKOTA TOURISM

became interested in the gardens, and upon her return she and her students began construction of a Shakespearean garden to be used for cultural events. Emma and her husband, Clark, retired from the faculty in 1932 and built a retirement cottage by the gardens at 501 Alene Avenue North. They used a postcard of the bard's famous cottage in Stratford for inspiration.

Though the seminary closed in the 1960s, the people of Wessington Springs have maintained and improved the gardens and cottage, which is named Hathaway after Shakespeare's wife. In 1995 an English-trained craftsman was found to redo the thatched roof with water reeds. No one in South Dakota had a clue how to roof with reeds. The work took several years, but today the cottage looks more European than ever.

Plays, weddings, holiday gatherings, and a maypole dance are just some of the regular festivities. It is open for guests on summer afternoons and by appointment. Group tours are welcome, and you can even request an English tea. For more information call (605) 539-1529.

Gann Valley Giant
Wessington Springs

If ever there was a sheriff who didn't need a gun, it was August Klindt, who wore the badge for six years in the 1940s.

Klindt, who hailed from the tiny burg of Gann Valley in central South Dakota, stood 7 feet 3 inches tall at a time when a 6-footer was big. And at 325 pounds, the Buffalo County sheriff was no string bean. He was a gentle man, say those who remember him, but for obvious reasons he didn't suffer much sass. Sheriff Klindt preferred walking to driving, but his car was spacious enough because he removed the front seat and sat on the rear.

The Jerauld County Museum in Wessington Springs (120 Main Street East, 605-539-1620) has pictures of the sheriff, along with his big felt hat and ring. The curator says a 50-cent piece fits inside the ring.

Displaying the big sheriff's trousers
SOUTH DAKOTA MAGAZINE

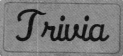

Gann Valley is one of the smallest county-seat towns in the United States.

The Blasted Namesake
White Rock

White Rock is a very tiny burg in the extreme northeast corner of South Dakota on SD 25. In 1884 practical pioneers established the town and named it after a huge white rock half buried in the center of town.

So you might think they would have built a flower garden around the big boulder. Or chiseled the town name on one side? Or moved it under a roof to protect it from the elements?

None of the above. The town's namesake was blasted to pieces, which were used for foundations of buildings. It was a bad omen in our opinion. The town grew to a population of 600, and then it dwindled to just a few people surrounded by many old foundations.

Best Place to Buy a Cap
Wilmot

"Why don't farmers wear tennis shoes?" goes a sorry joke in farm country. "Because seed corn companies don't give them away."

But even bad humor carries a ring of truth. If you doubt it, visit the Hanson family's Wilmot store: Sports Cards, Antiques & Collectibles (700 Main Street). Located in the town's old hospital, the store includes David and Del Hanson's extensive farm-cap collection.

"We must have over a thousand by now," says Dave. "It all started when I had a feed store called Hanson Feed & Semen. I gave away caps, and people would sometimes leave one. My brother was traveling South Dakota at the time, and we both started collecting caps." They displayed the headgear on wires when their huge antiques store opened.

Was it hard to place a value on the collection? Not at all, says Dave: $2 a cap. If you show up hatless (because you're a city slicker or because you haven't seen your feed, seed, and semen rep lately), you can take your pick. Or you can trade hats if you see one that better complements the jacket you got from your tractor dealer.

If the store is locked, you'll find Dave nearby at the First State Bank of Wilmot (605-520-3781).

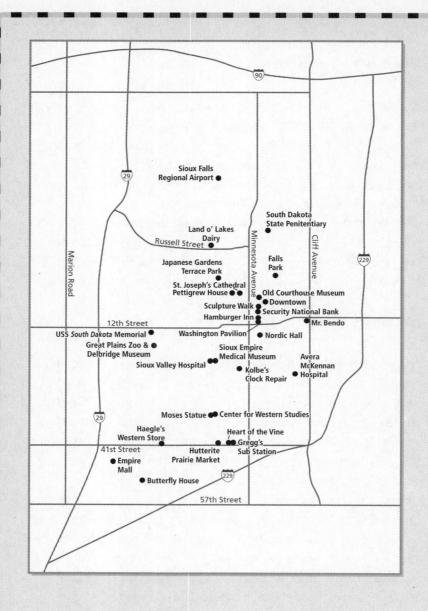

Sioux Falls Regional Airport ●

South Dakota State Penitentiary ●

Land o' Lakes Dairy ●

Russell Street

Minnesota Avenue

Cliff Avenue

Marion Road

Falls Park ●

Japanese Gardens Terrace Park ● ●

St. Joseph's Cathedral Pettigrew House ● ●

Old Courthouse Museum ●

Sculpture Walk ●

● Downtown

Hamburger Inn ●

● Security National Bank

12th Street

● Mr. Bendo

USS *South Dakota* Memorial ●

Washington Pavilion ●

● Nordic Hall

Great Plains Zoo & Delbridge Museum ●

Sioux Empire Medical Museum ● ●

Avera McKennan Hospital ●

Sioux Valley Hospital

Kolbe's Clock Repair ●

Moses Statue ● ● Center for Western Studies

Haegle's Western Store ●

Heart of the Vine ● ●

● Gregg's Sub Station

41st Street

Hutterite Prairie Market

● Empire Mall

● Butterfly House

57th Street

Sioux Falls

2

Sioux Falls

At 150,000 people *and growing, Sioux Falls is South Dakota's largest city, but the city doesn't dominate the region. Though it has been gaining charm and population, part of its allure is that it isn't becoming a bully or a braggart. Like a wealthy uncle, it's just nice to have around.*

Sioux Falls doesn't overwhelm South Dakota politically. Its citizens vote much the same as their rural neighbors, and though its legislators have grown in number with every official census, they haven't been a united force in Pierre because they hardly agree among themselves.

Culturally, the city isn't exactly the epicenter of prairie life. South Dakota's identity is rooted in the bawdy Black Hills, the displaced Lakota and Dakota Indians, the struggling farmer and rancher, and the plucky small towns. We prefer poems, stories, and songs about adversity and hard times. Sioux Falls doesn't inspire those popular themes.

Economically, the city has been a godsend of opportunity for thousands of young people who couldn't find work where they were born and raised, but their hearts stay in the rural beyond.

Certainly, Sioux Falls has become the entertainment capital for the farming prairie, with its fairs, festivals, concerts, shopping, museums, and restaurants. In the busy downtown area, city officials allow bars and eateries to set tables on the sidewalks. Compare that attitude to most of our small cities—where local leaders often won't allow as much as a bench on their wide and deserted main streets.

Lift a Car, Win Your Lunch

Let's imagine that you and your tightwad, know-it-all brother-in-law are driving to Sioux Falls to spend the day. Here's how you can have some fun:

You say, "Hey, cheapo, I'll bet lunch that I can lift a car up off the ground."

Cheapo looks at you cross-eyed and says, "What's the gimmick?"

"I'll lift a car up off the pavement."

"All four wheels? A real car?"

"Yup. Yup."

"Just you and nobody else?"

"Yup."

"With your bare hands—no forklifts, hydraulics, or cranes?"

"Yup, yup, and yup."

So you shake on it, and when you get to Sioux Falls you drive to the Washington Pavilion (301 South Main Street) and pull up to the curb—alongside a new car in a big metal basket hooked to a very long lever with a white, braided nylon rope attached. There's likely to be a sixty-pound grade-school girl pulling on the rope, thus activating a 35-foot lever and lifting the car high in the air. You win.

You could enjoy your free lunch right there at Leonardo's Cafe in the Pavilion, which is an amazing arts and science center housed in a castlelike structure that was originally built as the city's high school in 1908. After a new Washington High School was completed in 1992, Sioux Falls citizens voted to convert the historic building into a regional hub for entertainment, arts, culture, and science. Visit www .washingtonpavilion.org for a schedule of what's coming next.

World's Oldest Log House?

Only a silver-tongued lawyer could argue that the big museum at Eighth and Duluth in Sioux Falls is a 200-million-year-old log house, but that's exactly the kind of man who built it. R. F. Pettigrew was a skilled lawyer and politician who arrived in Dakota Territory as a young surveyor in 1869 and became one of Sioux Falls' biggest build- ers and boosters.

He started several dozen enterprises and made a fortune before losing a million dollars in the Great Depression of 1893. He served in the territorial legislature, and became one of the South Dakota's first two U.S. senators in 1889. He began his political career as a

These logs will never burn.

Republican, but joined William Jennings Bryan's populist crusade for silver in 1896 and later moved from the Democratic Party to socialism and then communism. He even corresponded with such Russians as Tolstoy and Lenin.

Pettigrew was an inveterate explorer. He excavated Indian mounds near Sioux Falls—a pursuit that would be considered grave-robbing today—and then traveled south when he heard of an amazing bounty of petrified wood lying unused in the Arizona desert. The stone logs date back to the tropical Triassic period, 200 million years ago. Pettigrew sent huge quantities of them back to Sioux Falls. When President Theodore Roosevelt discovered the damage being done by Pettigrew and others, he convinced Congress to create the Arizona Petrified Forest National Park in 1906.

Pettigrew intended to cut and polish his huge inventory of petrified wood and sell pieces to tourists, but the plan never crystallized. He later used some of them to build a huge arch at the Woodlawn Cemetery (26th and Cliff), and he added other chunks and slices as accents on his majestic Queen Anne–style home, which is just south of St. Joseph Cathedral in the center of town.

Pettigrew expanded the house in 1923 as a museum for artifacts and oddities collected by him and his brother, Fred. Today the Pettigrew House is part of the Siouxland Heritage Museums. Visitors are welcome seven days a week (free admission), but please don't take the logs, even if you're from Arizona.

Visit www.siouxlandmuseums.org for an online tour of the Pettigrew. For more information call (605) 367-7097.

Quite a Balancing Act

Nobody knows exactly how long Balance Rock has been tottering on a cliff's edge in Palisades State Park, northeast of Sioux Falls, but it's been about 1.8 billion years.

How could we know? That's the age of the Sioux quartzite.

Balance Rock in Palisades State Park

★ ★

Ancient earthquake activity and centuries of erosion probably left the rock in its seemingly precarious position.

Of course, it's a boon for photographers, who love to pose family and friends as if they're pushing the rock over or holding it up. Which pose they choose probably says more about the photographer than a Myers-Briggs personality profile.

Just upstream on Split Rock Creek are King and Queen Rocks, two boulders that rise above the rest of the scenic river valley.

Palisades State Park, one of the state's smallest parks, is a pretty place between Brandon and Garretson where you can hike, canoe, kayak, bird-watch, camp, or just enjoy nature. The park is just a short drive northeast of Sioux Falls; take I-90 east to the Brandon exit and go north on SD 11.

The Boy Loved by Birds

A gravestone at East Nidaros Cemetery near Baltic, west of Sioux Falls, memorializes a boy and his feathered friends.

While growing up in the Baltic area, little Gustav Solem could call birds down from the trees. They perched on his finger and sang to him. He loved the birds, and they loved him.

Sadly, the gentle lad became ill with scarlet fever and died March 23, 1904, at the age of seventeen. His funeral was held at the old Nidaros Lutheran Church in Minnehaha County. It was a fine spring day, and warm enough that the front door of the church was left open for fresh air. Suddenly birds flew in the open door and sat quietly on Gustav's casket. The family was awestruck by the avian display of affection, and when they designed Gustav's tombstone, they had a bird sculpted on the top.

✦ ✦

Turn Right at Mr. Bendo

South Dakotans are notoriously good at giving directions. Sometimes they'll even insist that you follow them. "I need to go to the [bank, post office, jail, whatever] anyway," they're likely to say. They might even invite you home for an iced tea or a quick bite to eat.

Contrast that with the story of the South Dakotan who was in New Hampshire and stopped at a fork in the road to ask for

Mr. Bendo is east of Daisy the plastic cow.

★ ★

Daisy is west of Mr. Bendo.

directions from a crusty old Yankee seated on a park bench. "Does it matter which road I take to get to the courthouse?" asked the South Dakotan.

"Not to me," was the curt reply from the Yankee.

Being experts at directions, South Dakotans will seldom use actual street signs as guideposts, even in our largest city. On Sioux Falls' east side, it's not unusual for the locals to refer to Mr. Bendo, an 18-foot-high fiberglass mechanic that serves as the mascot for Buck's Mufflers at 12th and Cliff. "Take a right at the giant muffler man and go 13 miles, and that'll be Minnesota," they might tell you.

At the northwest corner of Sioux Falls, a big Holstein cow named

★ ★

Daisy stands outside the Land o' Lakes Dairy building on Russell Street. Go west around the cow until you hit I-29 and then head north, and you'll eventually reach North Dakota. Go south for Iowa and Nebraska. Go east and you'll see Mr. Bendo. What else could you need to know?

America's other great cities should erect a few fiberglass landmarks.

The Waterfall Got No Respect

Waterfalls are rare spectacles on the Northern Plains. Sioux Falls took its very name from the scenic rock falls on the Big Sioux River, so you would think that place would be as sacred, on a smaller scale, as Lake Michigan is to Chicago or the Rocky Mountains are to Denver.

Fortunately, Sioux Falls' early leaders weren't running Denver, or the Rockies might have been trimmed down to hills. That's exactly what they did to the waterfalls.

In the 1920s they permitted the power company to shave the lower falls, quite substantially, so the river would flow more smoothly into the company's hydroelectric plant. Years later they realized people liked to picnic, flirt, or walk their dogs past the falls—and they've been compensating for their mistake ever since.

Trivia

Adam Winrich cracked a bullwhip 261 cracks in a minute, setting a record at the Spirit of the West Festival in Sioux Falls on September 17, 2005. It earned him a mention in the *Guinness Book of World Records*.

The riverfront is now a source of pride for Sioux Falls citizens. The city has created a beautiful forty-two-acre park. Historic structures add to the landscape, including a flour mill and the hydroelectric plant that caused such embarrassment. An old horse barn has reopened as an arts center, and restaurants, shops, and loft apartments are filling empty and underused old warehouses, factories, and depots.

The waterfall won't be dynamited again.
SOUTH DAKOTA TOURISM

✦ ✦

Why All the Banks?

You may wonder why Sioux Falls has so many banks, and why some don't seem interested in walk-in traffic. Why, for instance, did one locate in the alley behind a pizza joint? It's because this is the Credit Card Capital of America. Many of the banks don't really care if you open a checking account or apply for a car loan; people are sending checks to them from all fifty states and many foreign countries.

Millions of credit card bills are mailed monthly from Sioux Falls, and almost as many payments are received here. (If you get a bill and don't send us a check, you're likely to get a courtesy call from someone in Sioux Falls, so please pay on time—we really hate to interrupt your dinner.) Twelve thousand people in the city of 150,000 work in the credit card industry, and one-fourth of them work for Citibank, which started it all.

When the South Dakota state legislature removed all limits on interest rates in 1980, Citibank hurried here to set up shop. Other banks followed—so many that they've had legal squabbles over such popular words as *First* and *American* and *National*. Wouldn't you actually appreciate the honesty of a financial institution that called itself the Three Hundred Thirty-third Hometown Bank and Trust?

Who You Gonna Call?

So you've got ghosts, but you don't want to spook them? Then don't call for a Dan Aykroyd type and his proton gun. Donna O'Dea, a Sioux Falls psychic, takes a gentler approach than was portrayed in Aykroyd's hit 1984 movie, *Ghostbusters*. You can reach her at (605) 361-9774.

O'Dea wields no crosses, carries no Bible, and doesn't believe in vacuuming the dead. "They're not evil," she says of ghosts. "They're just lost." She helps them understand that it's time to leave the earthly life and move on to the next world.

She's never scary, not even to angry spirits. "OK, you guys need to quit!" she told the ghosts of a U.S. cavalry soldier killed at the Little Bighorn in 1876 and the Lakota warrior who killed him and then died

★ ★

at Wounded Knee in 1890. They were causing a ruckus in the basement of a Canton restaurant. "Custer lost," she told them both. "It's the year 2001. It's over. The fight is over."

O'Dea stepped between the two spirits and said, "See, you can't punch me. You can't hurt me. My body is alive. The blood is over. The pain is over. The war is over. Work for peace on the other side."

Finally, she demands "Go!" Most ghosts don't know they're dead, she explains. Hmm . . . have people been ignoring you lately?

The Scene of the Crime

At Ninth and Main in downtown Sioux Falls, crime history aficionados can saunter under the same marble bank pillars that John Dillinger raced past on March 6, 1934, while withdrawing $49,000 from Security National Bank.

Since Dillinger didn't have an account, a teller rang the alarm and police converged on the gang. Leroy "Baby Face" Nelson wounded a patrolman as they made their escape. The robbers forced five bank employees to stand on the running boards of their getaway car (a stolen white Packard) and headed for Minnesota. They scattered

Fudge by Faith

Should you have the misfortune of being behind bars in South Dakota, the only sweet part will come on Christmas Eve, when you'll receive some fudge in a bag of goodies. Prison chaplains collect the fudge, which is cooked by volunteers who follow a warden-approved recipe. The penitentiary has about 2,900 prisoners, and there always seems to be just enough. "The fudge is by faith," says Reverend Regan Beauchamp.

roofing nails on the road to deter lawmen from following.

The hostages were released unharmed and the patrolman recuperated from four bullet wounds, but the $49,000 was never recovered. Dillinger was considered Public Enemy No. 1 at the time by federal authorities, and Sioux Falls was an easy mark for him.

The Security National building still stands, but don't get any dumb ideas—it's just offices and apartments today. The big money is a block east on Phillips Avenue.

Hard Time: A Granite Prison

We hope you never need to try, but South Dakota's state penitentiary in Sioux Falls appears inescapable—especially if you plan to burrow through the walls, because they're built of Dakota quartzite. The pink stone, which is native to the Big Sioux River Valley, is malleable when first dug from the ground, but once exposed to air, it becomes one of the hardest granites on earth—bad news if you break the law in South Dakota.

The state's first prisoners helped build the granite penitentiary in the 1880s. Razor wire, electrical deterrents, and a few other modern contraptions have been added through the years, but the structure still looks like a pink castle overlooking downtown Sioux Falls and the picturesque Falls Park.

Is it inescapable? Well, a few prisoners have found their way out—but never by digging or blasting through the walls. The biggest prison break happened in 1922, when four men jumped a deputy warden, took his keys, and unlocked an entire cell block. The other prisoners decided to stay where they were, but the foursome exited the pink walls and commandeered a tourist's car. They fled on back roads, west across South Dakota. Ten days later a posse caught them. One was killed in the confrontation, and the other three went back to the prison.

Behave yourself in South Dakota and you'll never get an interior view of the castle; but for an exterior look, take either Minnesota or Cliff Avenues to North Avenue and follow it to the top of the hill.

★ ★

The Battleship *South Dakota*

What must a warship do to stay afloat? The most decorated vessel in World War II—and the first to fire on Japan—was sold for scrap metal in 1962.

It was an inglorious end to a storied career. The USS *South Dakota* was built at the Camden, New Jersey, shipyard in 1939 and launched in June 1941. It fought in every major sea battle of the Second World War and played an important role in the Battle of Santa Cruz Islands.

The USS *South Dakota* is like a ghost ship.
SOUTH DAKOTA MAGAZINE

It received thirteen battle stars, the most of any ship in WWII. Forty-two of its sailors died in the war.

South Dakotans wanted to save their famous battleship from the disgrace of the scrap heap—but how do you sail a 35,000-ton ship across Iowa and Illinois? So they did the next best thing: They made a concrete border of the boat in its exact proportions (680 by 108 feet). You can walk the deck and enter a small museum that includes actual memorabilia.

Too many war memorials are just a flag and a stone. This one is unique. It's hard to do justice to a brave battleship, but the stark outline in grass—more than a thousand miles from any suitable dock—gives an aura of a ghost ship far from home but enjoying a deserved rest.

The "ghost ship" lies in Sherman Park at Twelfth and Kiwanis.

Follow Your Nose

Looking for a lutefisk feed? If you're a Norwegian, just follow your nose. If you're not, follow a Norwegian.

The feeds aren't hard to find in the Sioux Falls area, where a third of the population has Scandinavian roots. Lutefisk is a favorite culinary tribute to the Old Country. Many Lutheran churches and other organizations celebrate with lutefisk feeds, usually in autumn and winter.

Some people insist they love it; others hold their nose and take a bite for tradition's sake. The trick is to douse it in hot butter. If you really can't stomach the delicacy, but want to be polite, here's a tip: Take a piece of lefse, put some lutefisk in one half, and roll it up . . . then eat the half without the lutefisk.

If you won't eat lutefisk, the feeds are still a treat. Swedish meatballs are often served as a side dish, along with other Scandinavian delights. And the jokes are great. Do you know how to cook lutefisk? Put it on a pine board, flatten with a cleaver, sprinkle with pepper and salt, pour on melted butter, allow to cool, throw away the lutefisk, eat the pine board.

★ ★

A few years ago a fellow called the Sioux Falls extension office and asked how to get a family of skunks out from under his front porch. The county agent told him to throw a few plates of lutefisk under the steps. The man did so. A week later he called the agent again and reported that the skunks had left. "But what can I do to get rid of all the Norwegians?" he asked.

Uncle Torvald (aka Bob Johnson), the region's favorite Norwegian comedian, frequents the feeds at Nordic Hall in Sioux Falls. He

**Sioux Falls humorist Bob "Uncle Torvald"
Johnson and a young friend at a lutefisk feed**

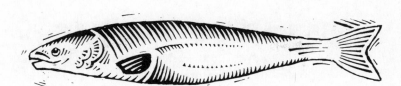

generously doles out tickets for a free lutefisk supper: all you can eat, all the trimmings, not valid Monday through Friday, void weekends.

Nordic Hall holds several lutefisk feeds during the fall; call (605) 322-9750 for details.

Lions in Aisle Five

Imagine coming face-to-face with a gorilla in the furnace filters aisle at the hardware store, but it happened to customers every day at West Sioux Hardware and Grocery. Henry Brockhouse, the proprietor, was an avid hunter. He traveled the world for forty years, bagging animals from five continents.

His Sioux Falls customers considered the collection quite a novelty. They referred to it as "the store with the stuffed animals."

Brockhouse died in 1978. When the store closed in 1981, some Sioux Falls citizens worried that the collection might leave the city, so a bond issue was proposed to raise funds to build an addition to the Great Plains Zoo. In conservative South Dakota, where school buildings and sewer systems have been lost at the ballot box, voters approved creation of the Delbridge Museum of Natural History.

Today the hardware store gorilla looks, well, almost human. A ghost-white polar bear seems fearsome. Leopards, walruses, striped tigers, and a massive African elephant (the skin alone weighed 800 pounds) reside in air-conditioned comfort, far from the jungles, deserts, and plains they once roamed.

Find the zoo and museum at 805 Kiwanis Avenue, a short drive north of the Empire Mall at 41st Street and I-29. For more information check www.gpzoo.org or call (605) 367-7059.

Some Other Good Lutefisk Feeds in South Dakota:

- Brookings—Swiftel Center, mid-October; (605) 695-6737

- Centerville—Old Street Cafe serves lutefisk in the months with an *r* in the name; (605) 563-3600

- Clark—St. Paul Lutheran Church, late October; (605) 532-3784

- Volga—Lake Campbell Lutheran Church, December; (605) 693-4328

- Lake Preston—Lake Preston Lutheran Church, February; (605) 847-4587

- Renner—Renner Lutheran Church, October; (605) 338-7120

I'll take mine rubbery and rare.

Flowers, Candy, or Lepidoptera?

Every travel book should have a few tips on where to impress your beloved. South Dakota has ample lakeshores and mountain retreats, but here's something unique: Show your sensitive side by accompanying her through the lep house in Sioux Falls, otherwise known as the Sertoma Club Butterfly House.

You'll stroll through a very large, indoor tropical garden with a gurgling stream. Hundreds of paper kites, striped oranges, owls, blue morphos, and other species of lepidoptera (moths and butterflies) are fluttering about. Wear bright-colored or white clothing and the leps are likely to land on your shoulders, maybe even on your nose. Whatever you do, don't swat at them—that'll spoil the moment.

The Butterfly House in Sioux Falls
SOUTH DAKOTA MAGAZINE

★ ★

Homo sapiens of all ages enjoy the lepidoptera, whether they're trying to show they have an appreciation for beauty and nature, or they actually do appreciate fine and fluttery things.

The Butterfly House is at 4320 Oxbow Avenue on Sioux Falls' south side. Call (605) 334-9466 for more information.

Sixteen Very Green Murals

The Old Courthouse Museum in downtown Sioux Falls doesn't seem, at first glance, like a place where money was ever in short supply. Built as a pioneer courthouse, the pink quartzite building has a steepled clock tower, 30-foot ceilings finished in coral and turquoise, massive ornate wood stairways, elaborate chandeliers, and wood floors that creak, as if to remind you of the history that continues to occur here.

The courthouse has sixteen murals painted around 1915 by Norwegian immigrant Ole Running. The artist painted South Dakota scenery, and he also added bug-eyed fish, castles, and other fanciful imagery. They are considered a wonderful expression of folk art, and they are quite green. Why green? Ronning was paid a paltry $500 for all sixteen, and it seems that green was the cheapest paint color at the time, so he laid it on thick.

The Old Courthouse at Sixth and Main is a professional museum, but run with some flair and fun. You'll like the permanent and changing exhibits and the gift shop full of unique regional art, literature, and merchandise.

Visit www.siouxlandmuseums.org for more information.

Hunting for *Shibui*

Most of this book is devoted to the wild, raucous, and eccentric side of South Dakota. The opposite of all that is *shibui,* and we have that, too.

There's no simple English translation for *shibui,* and it is not easily discovered at a rodeo, turtle race, pheasant hunt, or buffalo roundup. In fact, it can't easily be found anywhere, but the Japanese Gardens

Sioux Falls' original Japanese Gardens date to 1928.
SOUTH DAKOTA TOURISM

★ ★

in Terrace Park were designed—with stone, water, and greenery—to help you succeed.

The original Japanese Gardens were built between 1928 and 1936 by Joseph Maddox, a city parks worker who had studied Japanese landscaping. *Better Homes and Gardens* honored his work in 1934 with its highest award for civic projects. But when Maddox left the city's employ to start his own greenhouse, his gardens fell victim to vandals and to disrepute from the anti-Japanese feelings of World War II.

In the 1980s Sioux Falls citizens took renewed interest in Maddox's work. Koichi Kawana, a renowned landscape architect from Japan, was recruited to oversee the restoration. The result is one of America's finest Asian-style gardens, here in the heart of cowboy country.

We know—you still want us to interpret *shibui*. It's a feeling, they say, one that comes from the austere, subdued, quiet, simple, thoughtful, unassuming, restrained, peaceful, and contemplative. That's the best we can do, other than suggesting that you visit the gardens in Terrace Park, located south of Russell Street by Covell Lake.

For more on the gardens or other Sioux Falls attractions, visit www.siouxfallscvb.com or call (800) 333-2072.

Skyline Steeples

Tour the grand St. Joseph Cathedral, mother church of the Catholic Diocese of Sioux Falls. Emmanuel Masqueray, a Frenchman who gained great fame in America by designing the 1904 World's Fair in Street Louis, was the architect for the Sioux Falls church. Finished just after Masqueray's death in 1917, its twin steeples tower over downtown from Duluth Avenue.

Masqueray's design was Classic Romanesque and French Renaissance—rare in this part of the world. The cathedral doors are open daily until midafternoon when the janitorial crew finishes their work. Contact the chancery staff (next door) for a guided tour, or call (605) 336-7390 to make an appointment.

St. Joseph Cathedral, a skyline masterpiece

The surrounding neighborhood, called the Sioux Falls Historic District, features the city's grandest old homes. Tuthill House (just south of the Cathedral) is now the bishop's residence. The Pettigrew House (131 North Duluth), home to the state's first full-term U.S. senator, is a picturesque museum of territorial memorabilia, oddities, and artifacts.

The city publishes a map and guide to the historic district, available at visitor information stops.

State's Oldest Speed Bumps

Sioux Falls doesn't have as many cobblestone streets as some cities its age, but it may have the roughest. See for yourself on Sixth Street (it's easy to find, just below St. Joseph Cathedral), where the pavers are cut from the Big Sioux River's ultrahard pink quartzite. A few meek attempts by city officials to remove the stones were thwarted

Slow down on Sixth Street.

by a coalition of historic preservationists, neighborhood residents who like the way the stones slow traffic to a crawl, and the South Dakota Wheel Alignment Association.

The Unforgettable Iron Lung

When the polio epidemic hit the United States in the 1940s, few places suffered more victims per capita than the little city of Lennox, just south of Sioux Falls. A mother awoke one morning, paralyzed on her right side; she was the third of her family stricken in a week. Three children were diagnosed after enjoying the same Sunday dinner. A baby was born to a young woman while she was inside an iron lung; it was believed to be the first such birth in the United States. Medical specialists traveled to Lennox to study why the community was so unlucky, but no cause was determined.

Because Sioux Valley Hospital in Sioux Falls had so many young polio victims, teachers were hired for their schooling. Some polio victims had to lie in iron lungs for weeks or months; for others it became a lifelong necessity. Only the patient's head protruded from the big steel tank.

That grim period in history is remembered at the Sioux Empire Medical Museum in Sanford Hospital, 1100 South Euclid. Founded by nurses, the museum has an iron lung and other memorabilia and exhibits from the early years of medicine in South Dakota. Billionaire philanthropist T. Denny Sanford donated $400 million to the hospital, and by coincidence it has been renamed Sanford Health.

The museum is open weekdays. Use the hospital's main entrance. For group tours call ahead to (605) 333-6397.

Dragons on Phillips Avenue

Who knows what you'll see on Phillips Avenue: nudes, farmers, waterfowl, dogs—even Einstein hung out one summer.

It's called the Downtown Sculpture Walk, and it was established in

2004. Sculptors of regional and national repute are invited to submit works that are sponsored by businesses and exhibited on the street. An all-time favorite was the smoking dragon, strategically set outside Stogeez Cigar Lounge. Dragons have been popular on Phillips.

All the sculptures are tasteful, so bring the family. They range from the abstract to some so realistic that you almost say "Hello!" Visitors can vote for their favorites, and each year's winning piece is purchased as part of the city's permanent collection.

The Downtown Sculpture Walk

★ ★

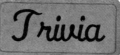

Trivia

There are many unique shops on Sioux Falls' busy 41st Street, called by some people "South Dakota's Main Street." Enjoy the fresh leather aroma and try on a cowboy hat at Haegle's Western Store (2800 West 41st), which grew from a 1910 harness shop, and dine at Gregg's Sub Station (1000 West 41st), an independent fast-food place that thrives due in part to great breads called Fun Buns.

New sculptures are unveiled in May and stay on exhibit all four seasons. You can find a virtual tour at www.dtsf.com/sculpturewalk. To learn more about downtown Sioux Falls activities and events, call (605) 338-4009.

Burger Lover's Hangout

A food critic visited the twelve-stool Hamburger Inn on East 10th Street a few years ago and said he loved it because "all the grease drained away by a George Foreman Grill is left on the burgers." It's hard to argue with success: Hamburger Inn is Sioux Falls' oldest eatery, dating to the 1930s.

Oh, it is changing a little. Longtime proprietor Nels Nelson was known for tiny burgers on tiny buns, and regular customers ordered sacks full. These days the burgers are larger, but they are still hand-formed and cooked fresh and juicy.

Chocolate malts, french fries, onion rings, and burgers make up the core of the menu—but an old tradition continues. The Egg-burger, a staple since Nelson first slapped a fried egg on a burger in the 1970s, is as popular as ever. Tell the cook to hold the burger, and you'd have a vegetarian option at the Hamburger Inn (111 East 10th).

The burger shop's phone number is (605) 332-5412.

★ ★

It's a Long Way to Florence

The original *David* stands in the Pizzale Michelangelo in Florence,
Italy, so it may be handier for you to see America's only full-scale
bronze replica at Fawick Park in downtown Sioux Falls.

Thomas Fawick, an industrialist who invented the nation's first
four-door car in a Sioux Falls garage, donated replicas of Michelangelo's *Moses* and *David* to Augustana College and the city of Sioux
Falls. For years South Dakota's *David* was controversial because he's
nude. Many people thought he should be hidden away. A Baptist
leader called it "an ungodly, vulgar piece of junk." Another pastor
said, "In the years to come, we can expect to see on the streets of
Sioux Falls people going naked. We can expect immoral acts in the
parks." Pranksters liked to diaper *David* or add fig leaves.

Moses was more easily accepted; it stands at Augustana College,
where you'll also want to visit the Center for Western Studies to see
a Plains Indian prayer wheel in the shape of a 50-foot tepee. CWS
has many exhibits of pioneer and Native American history, art, and
culture. It also has a gift shop and bookstore. Call (605) 274-4007, or
visit the center online at www.augie.edu/CWS.

Sioux Falls citizens now seem to take a more liberal attitude
toward sculpture as an art form. Public nudity is still frowned upon,
but Michelangelo no longer gets all the blame.

David was a popular scapegoat.

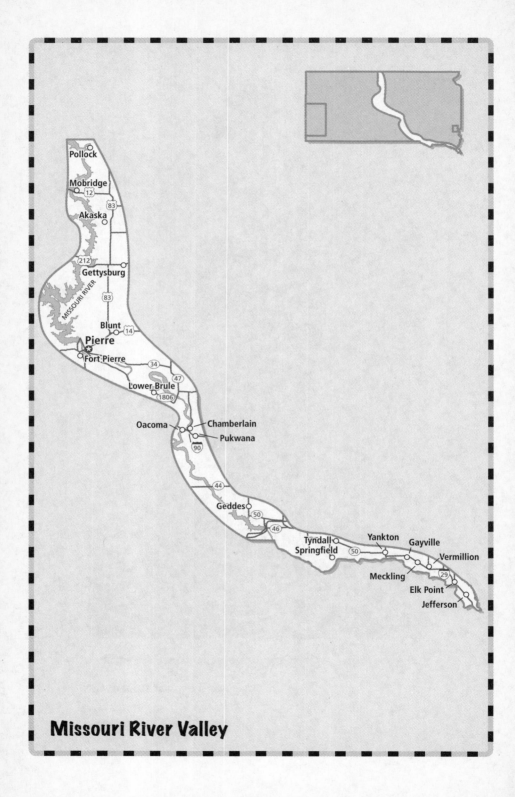

Missouri River Valley

3

Missouri River Valley

America's beloved humorist *Mark Twain spent a little time in South Dakota, and perhaps that's where he developed the maxim "Whiskey's for drinking, water's for fighting."*

The Missouri River has been at the center of controversy and adventure at least since Lewis and Clark explored its valley in 1804. Everybody has an opinion on the "Muddy Mo," the world's eighth-longest river. It would rank third if we could persuade mapmakers that the Mississippi is just its tributary.

The Missouri measures 2,341 miles. It exits South Dakota at the state's southeast tip, where the upscale planned community Dakota Dunes makes Union County one of the nine most affluent counties in the U.S. By contrast, some of America's poorest families live farther upstream on the Crow Creek, Lower Brule, Standing Rock, and Cheyenne Indian Reservations.

In retrospect, some Native Americans wish they had implemented a tougher immigration policy after Lewis and Clark showed up, because they too love the Missouri. Today farms, ranches, golf courses, hunting lodges, fishing resorts, and other developments follow the river on its northwesterly course. It splits South Dakota into East River and West River, but it unites us more than it divides us.

★ ★

Super Bowl of Drug Busts
Akaska

Akaska is home to two dozen people until the walleye start biting, and then the population swells with anglers. The quiet village on the east shore of the Missouri is an hour's drive from Pierre—but your DC-7 can make it in ten minutes, and you can land in the grasslands near the river. It's been done.

On Super Bowl Sunday afternoon in 1980, some local men left their ice-fishing shacks on the Missouri and headed home to watch the game. About sundown a huge plane flew low over their heads. They saw it land about 3 miles away.

The fishermen followed with their pickups, thinking they'd seen a plane crash. When they neared the landing site, they saw a suspiciously undamaged plane. Two men in the plane said they had engine trouble; one of them muttered something about being low on fuel.

One of the Akaskans parked his pickup in front of the plane so it couldn't take off, and another ducked around the back of the plane and let the air out of the tires. Soon the two strangers fled into the night.

Local authorities eventually arrested six men and seized $18 million worth of marijuana in the plane—the biggest drug bust in state history. Apparently the plane had flown from Colombia to rendezvous with local dealers. They intended to land during the Super Bowl when everyone would be watching television, but due to a strong south wind, they arrived early and were spotted.

This is one fish story they don't have to embellish at the Sportsmen's Bar in Akaska.

Was There a Snake God?

Blunt

Mysteries are rare in South Dakota. Nearly every square foot has been trod by ranchers, sportsmen, hikers, historians, and archeologists. When something unusual is discovered—an ancient bone or shard of pottery—it's quickly explained.

But atop some hills are stone effigies of turtles and snakes, and nobody knows who made them or why. Rock outlines of turtles are the circumference of a small garage; snake effigies are as long as a football field. The effigies are atop Medicine Knoll near Blunt, Snake

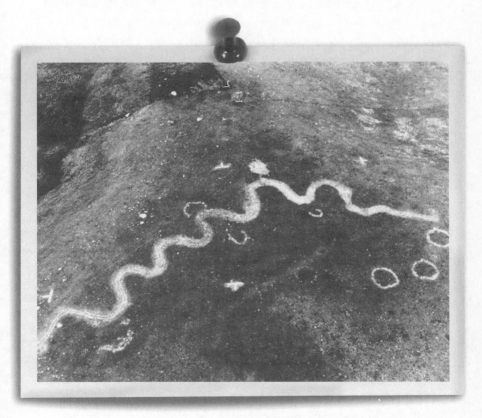

A stone snake, dusted in baking powder for the picture
SOUTH DAKOTA MAGAZINE

★ ★

Butte south of Harrold, and on other hills. A historical marker on SD 1804 north of Pierre commemorates the sites.

Archeologists think they date back 200 to 600 years. Native Americans were intrigued by the stone symbols before white settlers arrived. Vine Deloria Jr., a noted tribal scholar who died in 2005, had a special interest in Medicine Knoll because his great-grandfather Saswe survived a surreal experience there while on a vision quest in 1831. The story, passed down within Deloria's family, was included in his book, *Singing for a Spirit.*

Saswe prayed for two days atop the hill. On the third day his people could not see him, so a cousin, Brown Bear, was sent. Near the top he and his horse were surrounded by hordes of rattlesnakes. He lashed at them and continued to the summit, where a large bundle of snakes was writhing over Saswe's still body. Sure that Saswe was dead, Brown Bear made his escape.

As the tribe grieved, Saswe walked into camp. At first they thought it must be his ghost. Brown Bear asked how he had survived the snakes, and Saswe expressed surprise. He had no memory of snakes during the quest.

If you climb those hills, we wish you the same good fortune. Breathing, biting rattlesnakes are more common in the Missouri River hills than the mysterious stone effigies.

Learn How to Fall Off a Horse
Blunt

All the world's a stage,
And all the men and women merely players:
They have their exits and their entrances . . .

At the Korkow school near Blunt, a "prof" is likely to deliver a lecture with an occasional spit of tobacco. One of the outhouses is labeled COED. The student uniform is a big black hat, blue jeans, and boots. It's a rodeo school, and the only ceiling to the aspirations of the youths is the sunny blue sky of rural Hughes County.

The Korkow family helped pioneer the sport of rodeo in the 1930s. They began to raise rodeo bulls and bucking horses in the 1940s, and their stock has been at the National Finals since the 1950s. Their best-known bull was Hell Cat, a wild beast who relished opportunities to send cowboys flying. He is buried in the ranch's arena—the main lecture hall for the annual late-April rodeo school.

Tuition is only a few hundred dollars, a bargain compared to learning some professions. Degrees are available in bareback, saddle bronc, bull riding, and bullfighting. Rumors that the cost is subsidized by local chiropractors and orthopedists are absolutely false.

Jim Korkow, the man in charge, stresses safety. One of the first lessons is how to fall. "Be ready to tuck and roll!" the instructor yells. Protect your head, then get up and exit the arena like you're terrified so the judges think you just rode a really mean critter.

Perhaps that's what Shakespeare had in mind when he wrote, "All the world's a stage."

Contact the Korkow Rodeo School's admissions department at (605) 224-5607 for more information.

The Bill-Paying Pen Collector
Elk Point

People are apt to collect anything for no reason whatsoever, and good proof of that is Roger Bosse, the retired Elk Point farmer who has thousands and thousands of pens and pencils hanging on one garage wall.

"How many do you have?" I asked.

"You gotta guess," he said.

He did hint that a man can hang twenty-five pens to a foot.

I quickly calculated that he had about 240 running feet of writing instruments, so that would total about 6,000. "That's my guess," I said.

"Did you count those we haven't hung up?" asked a grinning

★ ★

Bosse, pointing to a half-dozen boxes and pails full. Most have advertising slogans. Some are shaped like ball bats, voluptuous ladies, and ice-cream cones.

My only other question was, why pens?

"Well, you know how it is when you go to town to pay a bill and you use their pen," Bosse said. "You say 'nice pen' and they say 'keep it,' so you take it home."

Farmers pay a lot of bills. Plus, when word spread about Bosse's collection, other debtors donated pens.

Lying on the flat, fertile bottomland of the Missouri River, the Bosse farm is surrounded by big square fields of tall corn. His French grandfather homesteaded there in the 1880s. Members of the International Pen Collectors Society and others are welcome to come see the pen collection. Call ahead: (605) 966-5678.

Roger Bosse will ask you to guess.

Trivia

Elk Point is called the Birthplace of Democracy west of the Mississippi because an election was held there on August 22, 1804, by the Lewis and Clark expedition to elect a replacement for Sergeant Floyd, the only casualty of the trip. The explorers, seeing a herd of elk, unwittingly named the future town when they called their camp "Elk Point."

Winning Ice Cream
Elk Point

Here's a scoop: Roman Emperor Nero was among the first to enjoy ice cream. His slaves mixed nectar with mountain snow. Marco Polo brought the treat to Europe; it came to America with the revolution of 1776.

South Dakota also made ice-cream history. Edgar Schmeidt added a marble-topped soda fountain to his Centerville drugstore in 1906. When his granddaughter Barb Wurtz and her husband, Kevin, added ice cream to their Elk Point pharmacy and gift shop, they restored Grandpa Schmeidt's antique parlor and called it Edgar's.

Grandpa Schmeidt came by to see his old soda fountain and gave a "thumbs up" to the Elk Point soda jerks. "Damn good malt!" he said. His biased critique spread by word of mouth, and soon Edgar's was a hit.

Now, when lists of favorite ice-cream shops are compiled, Edgar's is often in the mix. *Midwest Living* readers voted it No. 1, and Delta Airline's *Sky Magazine* calls it one of the five best in the nation, even though you can't land a passenger jet in this town of 1,900.

Sky's editors favored Edgar's Rocket, a vertical banana split. Really hungry diners do the Dirty Shoe, a brownie with vanilla ice cream, hot fudge, hot caramel, marshmallows, Oreos, coconut, and cashews. Is it any wonder that even *Gourmet* magazine raved about the little parlor?

Edgar's Favorite Malt is served in a glass, and you get the overflow in the mixing tin. You'll leave wishing you had a magazine to brag the place up.

Call ahead at (605) 356-3336 if you want to check on the flavor of the day, or drop by 107 East Main in Elk Point.

South Dakota's award-winning soda fountain

The Mighty Mo

The Missouri is the world's eighth-longest river. It flows for 2,341 miles through seven states, but it has only a few truly wild stretches, including a 59-mile jaunt from the Elk Point/Ponca (Nebraska) area to Gavins Point Dam at Yankton, and a 39-mile section downstream from the Fort Randall Dam at Pickstown.

The Missouri has been dammed multiple times above Yankton, and it has been channelized and stabilized below the Elk Point/Ponca area for barge traffic. The National Park Service is determined to hide humans' footprints as much as possible, so enjoy yourself but be respectful of the rare wilderness.

The (occasionally) wild Mighty Mo
SOUTH DAKOTA TOURISM

★ ★

The Doggone Missing Plates
Fort Pierre

Where are the missing Verendrye plates? Though this is not a mystery most South Dakotans ponder, it deserves some thought because the plate discovered by Ethel Roberts and her two friends in 1913 on a Fort Pierre hilltop is considered the oldest written record of the white man's arrival in the region now known as the Dakotas.

The last plate to be found (and lost?)
SOUTH DAKOTA MAGAZINE

The Verendryes buried one plate above Fort Pierre.
SOUTH DAKOTA MAGAZINE

King Louis XV of France sent three lead plates with the Verendrye brothers and their expedition in 1743. Their journals indicate that one was given to an Indian chief and another was placed on a hilltop by the river. No mention was made of the third.

The plate found by the children is on display at the Cultural Heritage Center in Pierre. A second plate was apparently found along the Cheyenne River in 1995 by Max Rittgers, a Madison native living in Florida. He was camping by the Cheyenne when he saw his dog urinating on something unusual.

The find caused a stir in historical circles. But Rittgers soon grew weary of the controversy over where it was found, who owned it, and where it should be displayed, so in 1998 he ended the dispute: He announced that he had flown over the Cheyenne and dropped the plate in the river valley where he found it.

Did he really throw away one of the oldest artifacts of white civilization in the Dakotas? Will it be found again? Where is the third plate? Bring your dog if you're interested in searching.

The plate found by the children in 1913 is now one of the prize displays at the Cultural Heritage Center in Pierre (900 Governor's Drive). The museum also has extensive Native American, Old West, and pioneer memorabilia and exhibits. Built in 1989 for the state's centennial, it is set into the side of a hill, like a very large earth home. For more information call (605) 773-3458.

Have Two Noon Lunches
Fort Pierre and Pierre

Never enough time in your day? Maybe you should live in the Pierre–Fort Pierre metro area, where a time zone (and the Missouri River) divides the two communities. Fort Pierre is on mountain time, and Pierre is on central standard.

Here's how that helps: You can rise at 7:00 a.m. in Pierre and fiddle around for two hours before you start your job in Fort Pierre at 8:00 a.m. Then you cross the river again for noon lunch in Pierre and get back to Fort Pierre at noon for perhaps a working lunch or quick noon nap.

Can't squeeze in all your afternoon appointments? It shouldn't be a problem here. You can schedule a 3:00 p.m. meeting in Pierre and then hurry back to Fort Pierre for another 3:00 p.m. meeting.

If you run with the party crowd, these are truly your kind of towns. Enjoy Pierre's nightlife until the state law's required closing time of 2:00 a.m., and then head west and enjoy another hour of frivolity until 2:00 a.m. MST.

There may be a glitch in this time-management plan, but we're too tired to think it through right now.

Fungi Food

South Dakotans are a generous people. We'll give you a ride, change your tire, write down directions, loan you money, and even reveal favorite fishing holes. But we don't even tell our own children about our best mushroom hunting grounds.

People who complain if they have to walk across the street to get a loaf of bread will eagerly trounce through brambles, weeds, and mucky creeks. They'll crawl on rotted leaves and climb barbed wire, all the while risking poison ivy, ticks, and mosquitoes. And for what? For the morel mushroom, which in reality is nothing but a fungus—and an unsophisticated fungus at that. Scientists say the morel is still evolving from its birth during the last ice age about 100,000 years ago. That's young in the world of evolution.

Morels grow wild in all regions of South Dakota, including the mountains and prairies. They thrive in wet, sandy soil, so the river-banks and tributaries of the Missouri are prime hunting grounds. No one has figured out how to grow the morel in a captive greenhouse or garden; they only flourish in the wild. Consequently, morels bring $100 a pound in some specialty stores. That's a lot of moolah for a genetic cousin to athlete's foot, green stuff on old cheese, and corn smut.

Morels usually appear in mid- to late April, depending on the weather.

Home of *Dances with Wolves*
Fort Pierre

The Houck family's Triple U Ranch is about as far as you can get from the glitz of Hollywood. That's what the Houcks like about it. It's also what Kevin Costner noticed when he was scouting North America for a location to film *Dances with Wolves,* his epic 1990 movie about a Civil War soldier who escapes to Dakota Territory and befriends the Indians.

Costner went to great lengths to show off the prairie scenery and the Native American culture. Indians in the area were employed to assist with costumes, language, music, and even horsemanship. Young Native Americans skilled at horsemanship were hired to ride in a chase scene for $25; the pay doubled to $50 if they fell off their horse at a dead run. On the first day of filming, a dozen young men were told to chase a wagon. A cowboy stuck his head out of the wagon and fired a single shot—and a dozen Indians fell to the ground.

Dances with Wolves was filmed at the Triple U.
SOUTH DAKOTA TOURISM

✶ ✶

Visitors are welcome at the Triple U, which has a gift shop and sells buffalo meat and other products like skulls, hides, and bones. Guided trophy buffalo hunts are even possible. Call Kay Houck at (605) 567-3624 for more information. The ranch lies alongside SD 1806, 31 miles northwest of Fort Pierre.

What's the Hay Capital?
Gayville and Meckling

The world's sweetest-smelling hay grows in flat, square fields along the Missouri River of southeast South Dakota. That's a boon for local farmers who excel at harvesting purple-flowered alfalfa at the opportune time and selling it for top dollar to dairy farms and horse ranches throughout the United States.

These farmers created a green economy before environmentalists ever invented the phrase: Growing hay is healthy for the land, the farmers, and the critters that enjoy protein-rich South Dakota alfalfa. But as with any successful enterprise, there is some strife; in this case, it's a rivalry between two little towns in the valley that are positioning for attention.

For decades Gayville (pop. 400) has billed itself as the Hay Capital of the World. Just a few miles farther east is Meckling (pop. 100), where the citizenry bills their town as the Hay Capital of the Universe. This is as confusing as when there were two football leagues (the NFL and the AFL) and no Super Bowl. Who's the real champ?

We could easily award a title if such championships were measured by tonnage, but quality trumps quantity in the NHA (National Hay Association). Gayville and Meckling farmers speak like white-coated scientists about energy content, protein levels, digestibility, and acid detergent fibers. They routinely draw core samples from hay bales with a probe and send them off to labs to be tested by infrared light.

Farmers from both towns modestly credit the river bottomland's rich, black soil and their mild growing season, but good hay also requires skill and hard work. It must be cut in early bloom and then

★ ★

dried to just the right level before baling. A little luck is also useful; a rain between the cutting and the baling might decrease the hay's value by 50 percent.

Neither town has been able to outdo the other in the field, so once a year Gayville hosts an annual Hay Days celebration that includes athletic competitions. Gayville and Meckling dueled in an annual tug-of-war years ago, but now their muscle-bound young men roll 1,000-pound round bales down Main Street.

Bragging rights are nice, but in the real world—with modern science and today's machinery—a pipsqueak with a good brain can grow good alfalfa.

For information on Hay Days (or if you have a hungry horse), call the Freeburg Hay Company at (605) 267-4426.

Meckling's claim to fame
KENDRA HENSELER

★ ★

Old Paps's Buried Treasure

Geddes

Some Charles Mix County historians think $50,000 in gold coins is buried west of Geddes, but you'll need scuba gear to find it.

Cuthbert DuCharme came from Canada to establish a fur-trading business along the Missouri River. He built a log store and operated a roadhouse tavern, and soon learned that the clean springwater on his property was ideal for whiskey-making, so he expanded into the liquor trade. *Papineau* is French for "whiskey," so the old trader became known as Old Paps.

Old Paps's log cabin has been moved to Geddes.
SOUTH DAKOTA MAGAZINE

When Fort Randall was established, Paps's Tavern boomed. Drinking, dancing, and wild partying went on all night long. DuCharme became one of the richest men in the young territory.

Rumors circulated about people who checked into the roadhouse for the night, never to be seen again. "Getting rid of someone every now and then never bothered Ol' Paps much," wrote historian Stanley Votruba. Especially vulnerable were gold miners and female homesteaders, lured to Charles Mix County by advertisements placed in Chicago newspapers.

Papineau married Theresa LaCompte, an Indian woman. As he aged he became paranoid about friends and family, but he trusted Theresa. At some point he gave her $50,000 in gold and asked her to bury it so they would have something when they retired. Soon after Theresa completed her mission, she was riding her horse when it spooked and dragged her to her death.

Old Paps buried her and then became obsessed with finding the gold. He dug and dug until he became a mental and physical wreck. Finally, friends committed him to the Hospital for the Insane at Yankton.

The gold was never found. When Fort Randall Dam was built downriver, it flooded Old Paps's land, so any treasure is now 30 feet underwater. Before the flood the citizens of Geddes moved his log cabin store into town, where you'll find it in the city park, well cared for and stocked with fur traders' memorabilia.

Medicine Rock

Gettysburg

A 10-foot boulder with five imbedded footprints is a centuries-old mystery.

Sioux Indians thought the footprints belonged to the Great Spirit, so they held ceremonies there. Lewis and Clark saw it on their 1804 journey. General Alfred Sully found it in 1863, and Lieutenant Colonel George Custer camped by it in 1873. Smithsonian investigators arrived as early as 1899.

Medicine Rock, before being moved indoors
SOUTH DAKOTA MAGAZINE

In 1925 Shield Eagle of the Two Kettle tribe of the Dakotas gave an Indian interpretation of the stone markings during a peace expedition at the site. He said a wise man inspired by the Great Spirit engraved the footprints to remind Indians that they are in the care of God.

White settlers planned outings around the rock. It was so popular that when Oahe Dam was built, Gettysburg leaders arranged to pull the eight-ton boulder into town so it wouldn't be flooded. For years it sat outdoors along US 212. Kids of all ages matched their feet to the rock's indentations. All that attention, combined with wind and rain, began to erase the ancient depressions, so the boulder was moved into a large room in the Dakota Sunset Museum (205 West Commercial Avenue).

Scientists believe the footprints were imbedded by preglacial men while the limestone was soft or carved by Indian artists. Your guess is as good as anybody's. One thing is for certain: We don't make rocks like that anymore.

Don't Drink the Fire Water

Early explorers with vivid imaginations reported seeing smoke from volcanoes in the hills bordering the Missouri River. Lewis and Clark, the famous explorers, heard about the phenomenon, so they investigated in August 1804 as they journeyed upriver.

"It appeared to have been recently on fire," wrote Captain Clark of the smoldering black bluffs about 8 miles below the mouth of the Vermillion River. He said a crevice was too hot to touch. Fumes from the smoke sickened his sidekick, Captain Lewis, and the men of the expedition also found they couldn't drink river water in the area without getting sick to their stomachs.

Nicollet, Fremont, and other explorers studied smoking hills south of Chamberlain, and they were soon dubbed the Burnt Hills, a name that's used to this day. The modern explanation is that oil and organic, coal-like minerals in the bluffs ignite by spontaneous combustion and can then smolder for months or even years. Though flames are seldom seen, the temperature within the crevices has been measured as high as 3,000 degrees Fahrenheit.

It's not a volcano, but it's too hot to touch—and Captain Lewis's warnings about the water are as true today.

We Know Who Wins That Battle

Gettysburg

Even though the North is always victorious, they keep refighting the Battle of Gettysburg in this little Potter County town. It's a wonder they're able to field a Confederate army after all these years.

The reenactment is an on-again, off-again event, but Gettysburg's fixation with the Civil War is permanent, because the town was founded in 1883 by grizzled Union veterans who came to Dakota Territory.

The Yankees camped at a place called Eagle Peak, the highest point between the Appalachians and the Black Hills (to which a Rocky Mountain dweller might say "Big deal!"). They staked out a town site 2 miles south of the peak and named it Gettysburg after the site of their bloody victory.

The Civil War colony had a population of just 200 in its infancy. The veterans started farms and businesses, and they were a fiery bunch, as neighboring Forest City residents soon learned. When Gettysburg won an election over Forest City as the county seat in 1884, the losers refused to hand over the records. The feud ended when the old bluecoats armed themselves and stole the safe and papers at daybreak. Nobody challenged them.

Many Potter County families still trace their ancestry to those Union soldiers. And even those who are not related—perhaps some with Confederate skeletons in their genealogic closets—are equally proud of their town's beginnings.

A cannon fired at the Battle of Gettysburg is on display at the town's Dakota Sunset Museum (205 West Commercial Avenue), along with other Civil War memorabilia. For information on the town and the reenactments, visit www.gettysburgsd.net or call (605) 765-2528.

The Grasshopper Crosses
Jefferson

This is a travel book, so we don't want to scare visitors, but the truth is that over the past 130 years we've had two major grasshopper attacks. Nobody died in either, so in the worst-case scenario, you'll make history if you are devoured by a horde of hoppers.

Still worried? Then keep to the Jefferson area in southeast South Dakota. Grasshoppers now avoid that area like, well, the plague. But it wasn't always that way. On a summer day in 1874, according to the local Catholic church archives, "as the people were coming home from church, they noticed a dark cloud in the sky. Some

A grasshopper cross near St. Peter's in Jefferson
SOUTH DAKOTA MAGAZINE

thought it was merely a cloud; some thought it might be cottonwood seed; but there was a chill in the hearts of those who feared the worst—grasshoppers!"

The sky turned dark as crops disappeared under the weight of the insects, which were described as shorter and grayer than your standard, garden-variety hopper. A girl was caught in the grasshoppers' path; they covered her body and ate away her dress before she reached her uncle's farmhouse.

The bugs returned in 1875, so early in the spring of 1876, Father Pierre Boucher (South Dakota's first resident priest) led his flock on an 11-mile pilgrimage. "It was a picture to be painted by a master," reads the archives. "The long procession being drawn through the deep mud, women and children in the wagons, the men and boys walking along the sides, the white-haired priest at the head and the entire company praying and singing as they made the pilgrimage around the fields whose crops had twice been devastated."

They erected three large crosses along the way. That summer the grasshoppers sailed in the air over Union County, and they haven't returned. Was it a miracle, or just coincidence? Local people obviously believe the former; they maintain the crosses and even remade them a few years ago when the old wood decayed. You'll find one at St. Peter's Church in Jefferson (400 Main Street). Another is 4 miles northwest of town on CR 1B, and the third is on CR 23.

Trivia

St. Peter's Church in Jefferson (402 Main Street) is a rural wonder. Built in 1891, it features Henry Goering's famous *Ascension* painting and other works of art, including *Stations of the Cross* from Canada. The church was recently restored.

Why Uncle Sam Demoted Big Bend
Lower Brule

Just north of Lower Brule, the Missouri River loops so wide that it almost completes a circle. River historians believe it may be the biggest natural meander of any river in America. A century ago, steamboats let passengers go ashore to walk across the narrowest point as the captain took the boat around the 20-mile loop. For years the place was nicknamed Big Bend, though some local farm families affectionately refer to it as the Pocket.

The river separates the Lower Brule Indian Reservation (on the west side) and the Crow Creek Indian Reservation (on the east). The loop's expansive innards belong to the Lower Brule, so its residents always thought it was literally a "big bend." Their cousins to the east, the Crow Creek, don't find the other loop nearly as daunting, so they call it "the little bend."

When the U.S. Army Corps of Engineers dammed the river at Fort Thompson in 1963, 7 miles downstream, government officials named the dam Big Bend and renamed the loop Little Bend to avoid confusion. The demotion, due to signage changes, worked for outsiders, but most local residents still call the loop Big Bend. The narrowest point of the bend is called The Narrows. They call the dam "the dam."

The best place to see a panorama of the bend is just 4 miles north of the Lower Brule community on Farm Road. Watch for a parking lot; it leads to a walking path that winds to the top of a high hill, and to a beautiful view of the unique river valley and The Narrows. We think you'll agree with the Lower Brule people that it's truly a big bend.

The Sound of South Dakota
Lower Brule

American music has become a monotone of sounds from Nashville and Los Angeles. Few performers successfully break away from the pack.

Paul (Summers) LaRoche was playing the "same old same old" at local gigs in Minnesota. But after his adoptive parents died, he

✦ ✦

discovered legal papers revealing that he was an American Indian from the Lower Brule Reservation in South Dakota.

He began a search for his roots and found siblings, an extended family, and a love of the land and culture that totally engulfed him. Along with all that came new music in his head. "That's where the inspiration came from," says Paul. "My life changed forever as I followed the road along the [Missouri] river to the reservation."

Paul LaRoche and his daughter, Nicole
PAUL LAROCHE

★ ★

LaRoche started a band called Brulé, and soon became America's top-selling Native American recording artist. Now he wants to use music to bridge the culture gap between Indians and non-Indians.

Brulé performs around the United States, but LaRoche makes an extra effort to perform in South Dakota, so watch for live performances—or listen to a Brulé CD as you travel the backcountry. The haunting, spiritual melodies seem to roll with the many moods of South Dakota's reservations, badlands, and prairies.

Brulé CDs are sold at most South Dakota music stores and bookstores. The band's schedule can be found at www.brulerecords.com. Brulé is featured every August at Yankton's Riverboat Days celebration, where the band plays nonstop all weekend in the shade of giant cottonwood trees near the Missouri.

A Color-Blind Toy Collection
Mobridge

Calvin Anderson played with scrap metal while growing up on a Campbell County farm near Glenham. "I'd push it through the grass and pretend it was a tractor and the grass was the corn," he said. "I never had a toy when I was young."

He grew up, married, and farmed with real tractors. He and wife Bernice didn't have children, but Calvin's love of farming prompted him to collect toy farm equipment. When the Andersons retired to Mobridge, they took along more than 300 toy tractors, bikes, wagons, and other miniatures.

Calvin wanted to share them, so he built a cabin for the town's Klein Museum, and that's where you'll see them today. Along with the toys he also donated actual farm equipment, including International H and M tractors and a 1902 Minneapolis Moline threshing machine, now used for grain-threshing exhibitions.

Some visitors to the Anderson collection may want to know more about the mix of red (International) tractors and green (John Deere) tractors, which represent a long rivalry—say Red Sox/Yankees, and sports fans understand. In South Dakota we don't argue religion, politics, or tractor color when ladies are present. Schoolkids, loyal to the brand their grandparents liked, still taunt one another: "John Deeres are green so they can hide in the grass when the real red tractors go by," or "Your dad drives Interjunkinals."

Calvin Anderson likes red but his father-in-law "went green," so he collected both. That should confound archeologists a thousand years from now. "I thought primitive farmers worshipped either one or the other, but never the two together!" one might say to a colleague as they excavate the Anderson cabin.

For information on the Klein Museum (1820 West Grand Avenue) and other area attractions, visit www.mobridge.org or call (605) 845-2387.

Fighting Over Sitting Bull's Bones
Mobridge

North Dakotans and South Dakotans waged a mini border war over the remains of the great Sioux leader Sitting Bull. The South won, and we ended the issue with twenty tons of concrete.

Sitting Bull was born in 1831, probably in the area now called Corson County. He was a great warrior and was among those who defeated Custer at the Little Bighorn. After the victory he led his people into Canada but returned in 1881 and surrendered. Sitting Bull was held prisoner for two years and then traveled with Wild Bill Cody's show. In December 1890 authorities believed the old chief was planning a ghost dance. They tried to arrest him, but he resisted and was killed in a brief struggle. Indian police quickly buried the body at Fort Yates, North Dakota.

Decades later, Sitting Bull's relatives in South Dakota felt the grave site was badly neglected. They also worried that the proposed Oahe Dam might even flood it. They enlisted support from community leaders in Mobridge, reservation officials, and even their U.S. congressman, but no one could convince North Dakota to return the body.

★ ★

Finally, on a snowy night in April 1953—sixty-two years after the chief's death—a group of civic-minded grave robbers from the Mobridge area sneaked into North Dakota and retrieved the body. Sitting Bull's wood coffin was rotted, but his bones were in good condition. The diggers carefully screened the sand to find even the smallest bones.

Their initial plan was to rendezvous with a small plane and fly the bones out. However, the weather was too thick for flying, so they

Korczak Ziolkowski's sculpture of Sitting Bull stands over the concrete grave.

drove the bones back to South Dakota, where a grave had been prepared high on a hill overlooking the Missouri River.

Twenty tons of concrete were poured on the vault. They didn't figure Sitting Bull was going to rise, but they did fear that someone from North Dakota might try to dig down. Armed guards watched the site for weeks. Korczak Ziolkowski, who had started the Crazy Horse mountain carving near Custer a few years earlier, carved a bust of Sitting Bull, and it was placed atop the grave.

North Dakotans made legal attempts to retrieve the bones, and they even filed a warrant for one of the gravediggers. Finally, they issued a statement that the South Dakotans had the wrong bones. Today all is forgiven between the states, and Sitting Bull rests in peace and concrete.

Visitors are welcome at the grave site, which is just 7 miles southwest of Mobridge off US 12. Pictures may be taken, but remember that it is the resting place of a great spiritual leader. Nearby is a monument to Sacagawea, the Indian woman who served as a guide and interpreter for the Lewis and Clark expedition.

The Chili Champ's Restaurant
Mobridge

If we had to review Rick's Cafe in twenty words or less, it would read like this: Outside is painted lavender. Inside, the politics are prairie progressive. The burgers, chili, and Indian tacos are incomparable. The owner . . .

Well, maybe we should start with the owner. Rick Christman is a former South Dakota Chili Cook-off Champ. However, unlike so many successful restaurateurs and cook-off winners, he's never coy about his best recipes. In fact, he once printed them on the backs of his business cards. He developed his own seasoning salts, but he sells the "secret seasonings" by the bottle to anyone who asks.

Rick is famous for his politics. He's not that far right or left, but customers who offend his sensibilities have been asked to

★ ★

leave—some for the night, some for two weeks, and others for life. He believes he's become more tolerant in recent years, but if you're really hungry, it might be best to talk about the weather, or fishing, or chili.

Rick's Cafe is located at 117 South Main Street; the phone number is (877) 540-5012.

Rick Christman and his colorful Main Street restaurant

Trivia

Not far from Rick's on Main Street is the Scherr-Howe Arena (212 North Main Street). Inside you'll find ten very large murals of Native American scenes painted by the great Lakota artist Oscar Howe as a WPA project in the 1940s. The murals rank among the great art treasures of the American West.

Where East Meets West

Oacoma

"East is east and west is west and never the twain shall meet," wrote Rudyard Kipling. Obviously, he never had a nickel cup of coffee at Al's Oasis in Oacoma.

West River meets East River in this sprawling family-run restaurant, gift shop, and store. Situated halfway across the state on I-90, this is where East River farmers and businessmen might share a booth and a laugh with West River ranchers and cowboys.

You might wonder how it all started. Well, Al Mueller was running a filling station along the highway—selling gas and tires and not much else. His wife, Veda, worried that he wasn't eating properly, so one noon on a summer's day when she wasn't teaching school, she took a hot plate to the station and grilled some hamburgers. Suddenly, she heard a customer's voice at the cash register. Apparently, the aroma of the burgers had reached the front. "Do you serve sandwiches here?" the customer asked.

Al said he surely did, and he went back and wrapped Veda's burgers in napkins and sold them. That's how Al's Oasis was born, and the Mueller family has been serving South Dakotans and out-of-state

★ ★

guests ever since. Yes, coffee is just a nickel. We recommend the buffalo burger and a slice of strawberry pie. After dining, you can shop for South Dakota books, art, and souvenirs in the Mueller family's big general store attached to the restaurant.

Take exit 260 off I-90 and you'll find Al's Oasis. Call (605) 234-6051 or visit www.alsoasis.com for more information.

Watch Your Step in Pierre
Pierre

You learn to watch your step around the capitol in Pierre (pronounced *Peer*), but not because of the politicians and lobbyists. They seem harmless. It's the geese that cause trouble.

During the legislative session in January and February, 105 legislators and about 400 lobbyists converge to decide what laws should be added, changed, or deleted from the books. The corporate lobbyists who fly in from other places find Pierre—the second-smallest state capital in the nation—to be an interesting seat of government. Cattlemen, cowboys, lobbyists, Native Americans, farmers, bankers, fishermen, and lawyers are all apt to share a breakfast table or a booth in the bar. As veteran lobbyist Bill Dougherty often says, "If you can't eat my steaks, drink my whiskey, and vote against my bills, then you don't belong in this legislature!"

Lawmaking is a major economic boost for the river city of 14,000 people. The next biggest thing is when the walleye are biting in nearby Lake Oahe. Consequently, Pierre's citizens excel at hospitality; they even tolerate hundreds of Canadian geese that live on Capitol Lake in the center of town.

The trouble with the geese is the droppings they leave on sidewalks and lawns around the capitol. You can always spot freshman lawmakers and out-of-state lobbyists because they are constantly checking the bottoms of their shoes and sniffing to see if there's an odor.

Geese and lobbyists are tolerated at the state capitol.
SOUTH DAKOTA TOURISM

★ ★

Trivia

Be sure to take a walk around Capitol Lake, where you'll find outdoor memorials and monuments, including the Fighting Stallions, which honors Governor George Mickelson and seven associates who were killed in a 1993 plane crash. A flaming fountain, fed by spring-water with a high natural gas content, is always burning. And, of course, watch your step while walking.

Our Longest Day Is in February
Pierre

Once a year in Pierre, the state legislature miraculously and legally turns a twenty-four-hour day into twenty-eight or thirty or who knows how many hours.

It happens on the last day of the regular legislative session, which occurs in late February or early March. The state constitution restricts the number of legislative days to thirty-five in even-numbered years and forty in odd-numbered years. But when the part-time lawmakers can't compromise on the last, pesky issues, they can always agree on one thing: They cover the clock at midnight (literally, with someone's jacket) and continue to debate, sometimes until dawn.

A few years back, the governor sued the legislature; he maintained that their final bills were not legal because the votes came after midnight. The South Dakota Supreme Court ruled that legislators can decide for themselves the length of a legislative day since it isn't spelled out in the state constitution.

The citizen legislature often provides high drama and colorful debate for travelers hardy enough to travel to Pierre in January and February. But that last, long day (usually late in February) is especially intriguing.

The clock in the state senate chambers is often covered on the last legislative day.

What's a Hog House?

Hog house is a legislative term unique to South Dakota. Many years ago the state agriculture college at Brookings wanted to build a hog farm, but it needed legislative approval and the deadline for bills had passed. Supporters took an unrelated bill and completely amended the language. It passed, and state lawmakers have been "hog housing" bills ever since. Deadlines are for schoolkids and chumps! If you got the votes, you got the power—that's the motto in Pierre.

★ ★ ★ ★ ★ ★ ★ ★ ★ ★ ★ ★ ★ ☆ ★ ★ ★ ★ ★ ★ ★ ★ ★ ★ ★ ★ ★ ★

Chipping at Oahe Days
Pierre

Oahe Days celebrate Pierre's river heritage. The festival, held on a weekend in July, features arts and crafts, food, music, and games like frog jumping and a buffalo-chip-throwing contest with a $20,000 grand prize.

The problem is that nobody really knows how to throw a buffalo chip (which, for the indelicate, is like cow #*&@ only bigger). More than 150 throwers competed in 2006 and nobody won. They threw them like Frisbees, baseballs, discuses, and footballs. Is there a better method?

Beck Motor Company, a local car dealership, sponsors the event. Jami Beck says more attention probably needs to be paid to selecting the right chip: "I recommend the heavier ones."

Jami and her coworkers collect a pickup box full of the chips from a buffalo pasture just prior to the festival. "We look for hardness," she admits. "You don't want them too fresh—but on the other hand, if they are too dry, they break apart."

Yes, this is a complicated sport, but it's in its infancy. Imagine how silly the first golfers must have looked. It took years before they came up with fine points like keeping your head down or wearing gloves to improve your grip. Hey, right there are two good ideas for buffalo-chippers.

If you're shopping for a pickup at Beck's, we suggest you closely inspect the box. For more information on Oahe Days, call the Pierre Chamber of Commerce at (605) 224-7361.

Where Romance Peaked
Pollock

It's embarrassing to lose a range of hills, but it happened east of the Missouri in Campbell County.

The Kiss Me Quick Hills were known well enough in the 1940s to earn a place in a popular reference book, *South Dakota Geographic Names.* They were also included in a 1973 revision, described as "a series of short, sharp rises in the road which almost cause a person to meet himself."

But the hills were nowhere to be found when a writer for *South Dakota Magazine* tried to find and photograph them in 2004. People in and around the little town of Pollock had never heard of them.

Only after a nationwide plea for information was it learned that the Kiss Me Quicks are three small hills, found about 5 miles east of Pollock. Byron Johnston, a Pollock native, wrote the magazine to note that the only way for Mennonite boys and girls to be alone was to take a buggy ride. When they reached the rolling hills, they could be out of sight for a brief time. This was when the boy said, "*Mich kubt schnell!*" You know the translation.

Have all the romantics gone away?

Stone Cold Love

Three stone idols thought to resemble a man, woman, and dog stand southwest of Pollock. Explorers Lewis and Clark saw the stones during their expedition. Native Americans told Clark a legend about a man and woman who were in love, but the woman's parents would not let them marry so the lovers, along with their dog, slowly turned to stone. The idols are in a remote area, so ask for directions at the West Pollock Resort.

★ ★

Made to Mow

Pukwana

South Dakotans love a race. We've waved checkered flags for baby pigs, wild cows, horses, tractors, turtles, cars, and grain combines. When we see four legs or four wheels, we want to know how fast they can go.

In fact, the nice little town of Pukwana was once famous for turkey races, and turkeys only have two legs. But when animal rights activists objected to the turkey races, the pace of life slowed in Pukwana. Then in 2003 two young men were driving their lawn mowers down a quiet street. One of them shoved his throttle forward and left his friend in the dust—and the Pukwana Mower Racing Association was born. There's no advocacy group for Briggs & Stratton engines.

Today the town's biweekly Saturday night races, held May through September, attract dozens of racers and hundreds of spectators.

On your mark, get set, mow!
LES VOORHIS

176

The races also deliver some much-needed economic development to the little farm town. Lawn mower racing is catching on around the world, but there's no venue quite like Pukwana. Helmeted drivers race around a small oval in an empty lot behind the Puk-U Bar & Grill on Main Street. Old tires border the track to protect spectators from the screaming mowers, which can reach speeds of 45 miles per hour. Mowers must have a shut-off switch that activates if a driver is thrown from the seat.

The mowers are divided into three classes: stock (nearly the way it came from the hardware store), modified (limited to 18 horsepower or less), and outlaw (limited only by your wallet or your wife's common sense).

Visit www.pukwanamowerracing.com for information and race videos. You may also call Brian Reis at (605) 730-2100. But to really experience the sport, spend a hot summer Saturday night in Pukwana. Bring your mower if you think it has a good high gear.

The Biggest Boat Dream
Springfield

When the river-loving people of the Missouri Valley dream, a boat is often involved. Such dreams come in all sizes, but usually they're well under 30 feet. Greg Stockholm's measures 68 feet from bow to stern and may weigh thirty tons when he finally launches it somewhere below Yankton in the next few years.

The aluminum shell of Stockholm's future sailboat sits on axles alongside his auto body repair shop in downtown Springfield. When he's not fixing car fenders, he works on the boat. "It's something I dreamed about as a kid," Stockholm said. "I made model boats, and then we built a little boat out of plywood and floated it out on the river and paddled around."

The son of a carpenter, Stockholm learned to work with his hands and his head. He has mastered the latest computerized metal-milling technology, and he also talks with ease about ship displacements,

Greg Stockholm, on the bottom of his boat-in-progress

water ballasts, keel weights, and other complex issues that a South Dakotan might never overhear at the local coffee shop.

Even when you build it yourself, a 68-foot boat is expensive. Stockholm has relatives in the Kansas City salvage business who keep watch for aluminum. He chose quarter-inch aluminum for the hull because he wants it to be able to survive "a whale ramming." Obviously, it's not being designed for the Missouri.

The plan (a carpenter's son always has a plan) is to sail around the world for a year or two. Then Stockholm figures he'll return to Springfield, and the boat, which will sleep twelve, can be used for cruises along the Atlantic Coast or in the Caribbean.

Until the launch you can see Stockholm's boat, alongside his shop at 811 College Street in Springfield.

Bon Homme's Eiffel Tower
Tyndall

The Eiffel Tower wasn't popular in Paris when constructed in 1889. A petition was circulated to stop the 1,000-foot structure, and some Parisians even wanted it torn down after it was built.

Apparently, news of the controversy never reached Tyndall. Only a decade or so after Gustave Eiffel's tower was finished for the

South Dakota's version of the Eiffel Tower

179

International Exhibition of Paris, county commissioners there voted to erect a replica on their courthouse lawn as a memorial to South Dakotans who fought in the Spanish-American War of 1898.

Nobody recorded, and nobody remembers, why the commissioners chose a tower across the Atlantic as the design for their 100-foot-high flagpole. Maybe it had something to do with the county's name, Bon Homme, which means "good fellow" in French. Historians think a French explorer gave the name to an island on the nearby Missouri. Bon Homme became a town in 1858, and a county by that name was organized in 1862.

Parisians have come to love their lofty landmark. The same is true in Tyndall, where the commissioners funded a paint job for their tower in 2005. Some farmers and homeowners think the only thing higher than the tower in Bon Homme County is their property taxes, so commissioners should feel relieved that the tower isn't any bigger than it is.

Zebrass, Zedonk, Zonkey?
Tyndall

What would you call a cross between a donkey and a zebra? In South Africa the question arises because both species are found there. But it wasn't part of polite conversation in South Dakota until Jeff Rueb added a handsome gray donkey with stripes to his small petting zoo on the edge of Tyndall.

Rueb also has alpacas, llamas, dogs, full-blood donkeys, deer, and a kangaroo-like wallaby from Australia that winters fine on the Northern Prairie so long as he has a heating pad for his long, thick tail. But the Zedonk is one of the most popular residents of the two-acre zoo with a cute red barn and white picket fence. The zoo is always open to neighborhood kids as well as out-of-town travelers. There's no admission charge, but you might leave a dollar or two to help with the grocery bill.

★ ★

The little zoo is at 19th and Redwood, but even locals who know the way will stop and ask at Tyndall Bakery (1707 Main Street), which was operated by Jeff Rueb's parents, Bob and Judy, for nearly four decades. What better excuse to try their kuchen, a German pastry pie, and lots of Czech- and American-style sweet rolls and breads? The bakery phone number is (605) 589-3372.

Bob Rueb, with the donkey-zebra cross

★ ★

The Magic Czech Chef

Tyndall

Eric Tycz is the proprietor, chef, and chief magician at the Sports-men's Rendezvous (1701 Main Street). He's apt to make objects stick to the ceiling, disappear, or show up behind your ear. And when it comes to cards, you'll swear he has X-ray vision.

Tycz has been cooking up tricks since age eight, when he got a magic set for Christmas. He had the knack, so he kept reading and learning. "I used the tricks to meet chicks in college [at the University of South Dakota]," he admits. But now he has an even higher calling.

Eric Tycz says, "Pick a card . . . any card."

"A lot of people say they don't believe in magic," says Tycz. "I tell them that what I do with cards or coins is really just an illusion, but when I get you to laugh, now that's magic."

Customers grin from ear to ear as Tycz turns quarters to dimes, empties a glass of water into his dry palm, and makes dollar bills stick to the 20-foot ceiling in his restaurant, which was built as an ornate stone bank. Pinned to the ceiling, surrounded by the dollar bills, are a few ladies' bras, leftovers from bachelorette parties. Tycz says there is no trickery, illusion, or sleight of hand involved with the lingerie. "It's just a Tyndall tradition," he said with a smile. A smile? Bras must have magical powers, too.

Tycz and his fun-loving staff are very serious about their menu. They serve noon and evening meals—including steak, chicken, and shrimp dinners and an occasional Czechoslovakian meal befitting the town's Bohemian heritage. The young illusionist always makes sure he has enough help on Friday and Saturday nights to allow him time to entertain.

Antonio Stradivari's Contribution
Vermillion

Antonio Stradivari died about 200 years before the first fiddle player even showed up in Vermillion and strummed "Old Susannah." Still, the great Italian violin maker is an important part of the city's culture because two of his violins, a mandolin, and a guitar are kept here.

The four instruments, built in the last half of the seventeenth century, are part of the National Music Museum, a world-class institution started by Arne Larson, a high school music teacher who collected old instruments. Just as Larson's huge house in Brookings was ready to burst at the rafters with rare and unusual pieces, the University of South Dakota welcomed him and his instruments to its Vermillion campus.

Arne's son, Andre, became director of the museum and has helped it evolve into arguably the greatest music museum in the world. Many pieces are extremely rare, even one of a kind. No one knows how many guitars Stradivari made (he's better known for violins), but only two have survived; one is at Oxford University in England, and the other is in Vermillion.

For a taste of the museum's expansive collection, visit www.usd.edu/smm—or better yet, visit the museum at 414 East Clark. Call (605) 677-5306 for information.

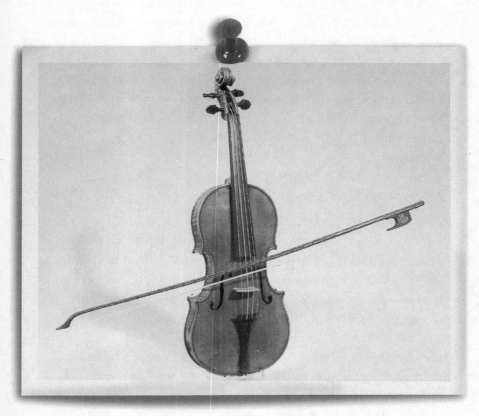

Not so rare in Vermillion
NATIONAL MUSIC MUSEUM

Sittin' on the Dock by the Bridge
Yankton

Yanktonians bought blocks of ice at the Ice House before the miracle of refrigeration. Now customers head for the old brick warehouse to cool off with their favorite beverage while parked in their car.

The Ice House is certainly South Dakota's only outdoor drive-in bar, and probably one of only a few in the country. On hot summer nights patrons arrive with motorcycles, cars, and pickup trucks. They either sip from their seats or hang out around a rustic, old wooden loading dock. Local custom allows you to smash your empty bottle under the dock before ordering another.

A late night at Yankton's popular Ice House

Since the end of Prohibition, three generations of the Anderson family have been quenching thirsts at this unique establishment along the north shore of the Missouri River in the historic downtown area. Almost daily, Jim Anderson entertains by repeating a can-crushing routine he once performed on David Letterman's "Stupid Human Tricks." He has stomped as many as 150 in a single quick-step dance.

Call (605) 665-2631 for information, or just park your car at 101 Capitol Street for a front row seat to one of the West's most curious bars.

Gentlemen, Crank Your Engines
Yankton

It's the slowest procession on wheels, paling speed-wise to South Dakota's more-famous Harley and Corvette rallies. But antique tractor parades are becoming a summertime tradition in South Dakota, and the granddaddy of them all is the Tri-State Old Iron Association's annual ride on the second weekend of July

The tractor-lovers gather in Paddlewheel Park near the Missouri River shores in east Yankton. Over the weekend, they embark on two long rides—one in Nebraska and the other in South Dakota. Tractors must be able to cruise at 12 miles per hour to qualify. "Remember, it's a ride, not a race," reminds the leader in striped overalls and a seed corn cap.

Many of the tractor owners are current or retired farmers who, as kids, probably grumbled about having to steer the tractor once around the North Forty. Now they ride all day just for fun. Some tractors are equipped with an extra seat for the wife or girlfriend. One enterprising fellow rigged a cushy sofa to his three-point hitch so "the missus" could ride along in style.

A few tractors appear as if they just came from the cornfield, but most look better than the day they left the factory, ablaze with the bright colors used years ago by manufacturers to differentiate their brands. In the evenings everyone is welcome to browse the tractors at Paddlewheel Point, where more than 200 will be parked in neat rows. The public can also see and hear the tractors at 6 o'clock Friday night when they parade through historic downtown Yankton.

To stay abreast of the Tri-State Old Iron Association's activities, follow the Web site of WNAX Radio, a pioneering farm radio station that went on the air in Yankton in 1922 after getting a license from President Herbert Hoover (www.wnax.com). WNAX is a major sponsor of the tractor ride. You may also call Rodger Harts (605-665-9785) for information.

More fun than farming

★ ★

A Church Built by Slaves
Yankton

South Dakota has cathedrals with towering steeples, and country churches with stained glass and marble statues, but few have the simple splendor of the little church at 508 Cedar in downtown Yankton. The AME (African Methodist Episcopal) Church was built in 1885 by former slaves. They migrated to Dakota Territory from the Deep South after being freed by Lincoln's Emancipation Proclamation and the Civil War.

You can walk on the same wood plank floor nailed together by its founders and take a seat on one of the original ten pews. A large wooden cross and a color picture of Christ are the only wall decorations in this humble house of worship.

The church is still used for weddings, baptisms, and other special observances, including Martin Luther King Day. Staff at United Congregational Church, located just down the block, provide care and maintenance for the old AME Church. Call (605) 665-7320 for a tour.

Landlubbers, Ahoy!
Yankton

Many first-time visitors to Lewis and Clark Lake at Yankton are surprised to discover 400 boats docked in the marina, and nearly half with masts and sails. Landlubbers have created a thriving little sailing community in the middle of the prairie.

The sailboats range from colorful little Hobie Cats to 40-footers with automatic sails and luxurious cabins. Smaller sailing ports on the Missouri have also developed at Lake Oahe and Lake Francis Case, but few ports in the West can rival the lake by Yankton, where summer weekends have a coastal feel. Lakeside eateries serve fried walleye, and sunbathers and swimmers crowd several long, sandy beaches.

Lewis and Clark Marina is 4 miles west of Yankton on SD 52 (605-665-3111). So "Come about!" as the captains say. Powerboats, pontoons, canoes, and kayaks can be rented at the marina and from other local establishments, but to ride the wind you'll need to hang around the docks and befriend a kind sailor.

Sailor's paradise in landlocked South Dakota
SOUTH DAKOTA MAGAZINE

The Amazing Light of Mary
Yankton

Visitors to Lewis and Clark Lake see three tall crosses atop the bluffs that border the lake. They were raised November 22, 1971, as the first step in what has become the House of Mary Shrine.

Local people still talk of that day. As each 50-foot cross was erected, a beautiful and colorful light circled the sun and then faded away. Three times the light appeared, once for each cross. The shrine's local leaders have no scientific or theological explanation, only a photograph that shows the phenomenon.

The outdoor shrine is always open for prayer and meditation. It includes a rosary walk, chapel, statues, and a gift shop. The uphill walk to the crosses is a hearty hike. Call (605) 668-0121 to learn more about the lakeside shrine, which is 7 miles west of Yankton along SD 52.

Watch for the three crosses.
KENDRA HENSELER

The Last Hanging
Yankton

A rigged jury found the infamous Jack McCall innocent of shooting Wild Bill Hickok in 1876 at Deadwood. However, McCall was retried within a year at Yankton, then the capital of wild Dakota Territory. He didn't find a friendly jury there.

"Broken Nose" McCall was declared guilty of shooting Hickok in Saloon No. 10, and he was hung by a rope in short order. Old-timers claim that when McCall's body was moved many years later, the skeleton had a rope on its neck and boots on its feet.

McCall's dastardly deed inspires vaudevillian theater in Deadwood and Yankton.
SOUTH DAKOTA MAGAZINE

★ ★

**The shooting of Jack McCall has been an inspiration
for artists, writers, and movie-makers.**

McCall's grave site is a well-guarded secret because Yanktonians
don't want their cemetery to become a trampled tourist attraction, as Hickok's burial spot did (Mount Moriah, aka Boothill, above
Deadwood). However, local historians can point you to the jail where
McCall was held and the brick building that housed his courtroom
in 1877. A few home owners like to claim that McCall is buried in
their backyard, but don't believe it. He's somewhere in the Catholic
cemetery.

The Yankton Chamber of Commerce had a billboard on the
north side of town that proclaimed WE HAVEN'T HUNG ANYONE SINCE JACK
MCCALL. However, as years passed, they found better things to tout—
Lewis and Clark Lake, Mount Marty College, historic architecture—
and McCall was all but forgotten.

For information on Yankton events and attractions, visit
www.yanktonsd.com or phone (605) 665-3636.

Going North? Take the Top
Yankton

One of the few double-decker bridges in the nation still spans the Missouri River at Yankton. The Meridian Bridge (so named because of its connection to US 81, the Meridian Highway, which cuts through the Americas from Winnipeg to Panama City) was constructed with private funds in 1924 and paid for with tolls until the debt was retired in 1953.

The bottom deck was intended for rail traffic, but a north–south train route to Yankton never materialized, so officials sent

Now you can walk across the Missouri.

northbound traffic on the top and southbound traffic below. The
towers were designed with hydraulic lifts so the bridge could be
raised to allow ships to pass underneath; however, ships have been
as rare as trains.

Automobiles and trucks frequented the bridge to the tune of
5,000 or more a day until a new bridge was completed just a
few hundred yards away in 2008. Historians and Yankton citizens
objected to having the old bridge destroyed, so in 2010 the states of
Nebraska and South Dakota cooperated on a plan to restore it as a
footbridge. Now you can walk across the wide Missouri without getting your feet wet. It's a scenic hike that connects to walking trails,
nature areas, and Yankton's quaint downtown district.

Sunken Treasure
Yankton

Riverboats steamed up and down the Missouri in the late nineteenth
century, carrying cargo and passengers to the fledgling port cities of
the Dakotas. These were fine, big ships, more than 200 feet long and
capable of carrying several hundred tons of cargo.

According to legend, a ship of gold bullion from Montana sank
near present-day Pierre. Survivors said the ship went down near three
large trees. Years later, the site was determined to be the three giant
cottonwoods called the Three Sisters in Griffin Park, near the corner
of Missouri Avenue and Crow Street today. Treasure hunters tried to
find the gold in the 1920s, but to no avail.

Some think there were valuables aboard the *North Alabama* when
it hit a submerged cottonwood trunk near Vermillion and sank. Locals
still call the river's curve the North Alabama Bend.

About thirty such ships are buried between Yankton and Omaha,
Nebraska. Several sank when an ice gorge moved down the river in
March of 1881. Giant chunks of ice squeezed and shoved the huge
ships to the river's bottom. The *Western* is submerged in shallow
water just east of Yankton.

Trains, trucks, and planes ended hopes of a riverboat resurgence. But some of the ships are still here; occasionally a sunken boat's wood skeleton becomes visible when water levels drop. When the *North Alabama* reappeared a few years ago, the guilty tree trunk could be seen at the front of the boat.

Steamers on the Missouri River were massive ships; some measured 200 feet long.
SOUTH DAKOTA MAGAZINE

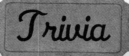

Do your best to arrive in Yankton on the third weekend in August, when city residents host Riverboat Days, a three-day festival of art, food, music, and fun on the banks of the Missouri. For details visit www.riverboatdays.com.

River Whales

Yankton

The paddlefish is the oldest animal species in North America. Some scientists think it is 350 million years old, more ancient than dinosaurs. Others say it's been here a mere 60 million years. No matter who's right, the paddlefish is prehistoric.

The spoon-billed fish, which can measure 7 feet long and weigh 200 pounds, is sometimes called the freshwater whale of the Mississippi and Missouri River valleys. It was once an important species for commercial fishermen, who valued the meat and also the eggs, which are caviar quality.

A single fish would travel 1,200 miles or more to spawn. However, habitat changes—especially the dams on the Missouri—have radically reduced their populations. Today in South Dakota they can only be fished below Gavins Point Dam at Yankton. Archers take aim in July, and anglers with snagging hooks try their luck in October.

Want to look a live paddlefish in the eye? Stop at the Gavins Point National Fish Hatchery and Aquarium, just west of Yankton on SD 52. You'll see the "whale" and a hundred or so other fish swimming behind glass. For more information on the hatchery, call (605) 665-3352.

Paddlefish are a remnant of prehistoric times.

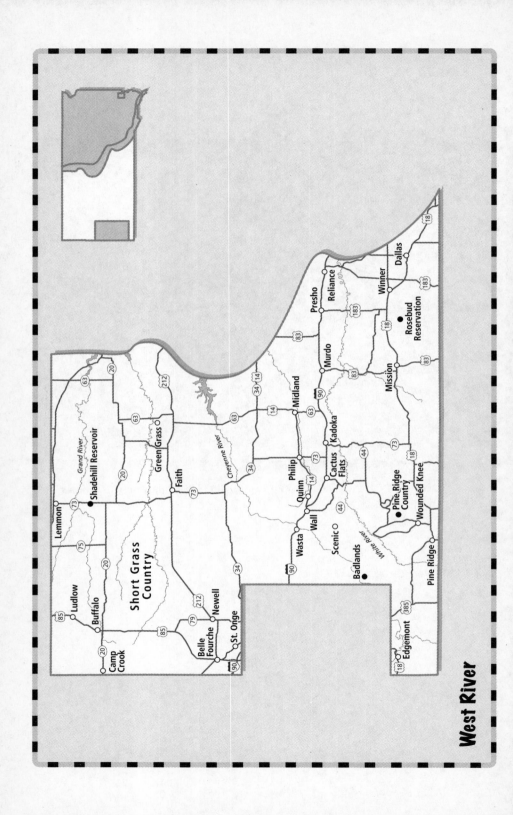

West River

4

West River

Cows, horses, and sheep all outnumber people in West River country. Still, the vast landscape is rich with colorful characters who seem to appreciate both their wide-open spaces and their next-door neighbors 10 miles away.

Such a man was Archie Gilfillan, whom we mentioned in this book's introduction. He was a Phi Beta Kappa who dreamed of running a sheep ranch while he studied Latin and Greek at the University of Pennsylvania. Soon after graduation, he arrived in Harding County in extreme north-west South Dakota. When his own ranch failed, he herded sheep for other ranchers, and he kept a journal of the land, the animals, and the crazy things people do. His journal is reportedly kept under lock and key at the University of Minnesota, and until it's released to the public, you'll have to rely on this chapter as a guide to West River.

If South Dakota is "The Land of Infinite Variety," it's largely thanks to the West River country. Without it, we'd look a lot like Iowa and Min-nesota. This is where the sandstone Badlands bloom above the prairie, where cows need twenty acres for grazing to survive a summer, and where men and women play the weather, the livestock markets, and Mother Luck, hoping to end the year with enough hay for the cows and enough cash to placate the bank.

Don't hurry across West River as you travel to the Black Hills. In this chapter are some suggestions on what to look for and how to enjoy what ranchers call the "short-grass prairie."

Watch Where You Drink
Badlands

Park rangers didn't get very excited when Stephen Gassman and Jim Carney tried to report that they'd found something interesting near Conata Road in the summer of 1993. Old bones show up regularly in the Badlands.

The visitor center was closed, so Gassman and Carney looked for somebody official to tell of their find. They finally saw a ranger at a campground, but she told them to report it on their way out of the park in the morning. They left for the Black Hills before sunrise and never had the chance. On their return trip they stopped again, and this time they met a ranger who knew more about fossils. Even he was only mildly interested until Gassman mentioned that they'd seen 3 or 4 feet of vertebrae.

As it turns out, they'd found an *Archaeotherium,* or "pig" for short. It was a prehistoric porker—the skeletal remains of a mammal that lived here thirty or more million years ago along with three-toed horses, saber-toothed cats, and hornless rhinos.

Watch for Ferrets

The black-footed ferret was once thought to be extinct. Fortunately, that prognosis was wrong, but the cute little weasel is still listed as the most endangered land mammal in America.

Thriving might be too strong a word, but a few dozen are alive and breeding in Badlands National Park's prairie dog towns, so keep your eyes peeled—especially while driving. We don't want to lose any on the road.

Amateur and professional archeologists, led by the South Dakota School of Mines and Technology in Rapid City, have been digging every summer since. They've even developed a Pig Dig Wayside Exhibit and a Fossil Exhibit Trail so park visitors can learn about one of the West's biggest ongoing excavation sites.

Why so many fossils in one spot? Scientists speculate that the basin was an ancient watering hole, and that some animals thirsting for a drink trampled others into the mud. Fortunately, West River's watering holes are not so dangerous these days.

For dig dates call (605) 433-5278 or check www.nps.gov/badl.

Is It Heaven or Hell?
Badlands

Lieutenant Colonel George Custer visited the Dakota Badlands in 1876 and compared them to "a part of Hell with the fires burned out." One wonders what he thought of the Little Bighorn, where he met his demise that same year.

The Badlands do have a parched and surreal appearance, but most visitors are more easily impressed than Custer. In fact, renowned architect Frank Lloyd Wright, who drove through southwestern South Dakota in 1935 after being invited by Governor Tom Berry to submit a bid for the design of a new Sylvan Lake Lodge at Custer State Park, compared the Badlands to heaven rather than hell. Wright later wrote:

> *Here, for once, came complete release from materiality. Communion with what man often calls "God" is inevitable in this place. It is everywhere around him and when the man emerges to the brown plateau and looks back, as I did, the sun now setting, a paled moon rising in darkening rose and blue sky as rays of last light drifted over, linking drifting water lines of dark rose in pallid creamy walls, gently playing with the skyline, with mingled obelisks, terraces, and temples more beautiful than thought, eternal . . . He will leave that place a more humble, seeking soul than*

★ ★

when he went in to this pure appeal to his spirit. He will know happiness in its higher than sectarian sense.

Wright lost the Sylvan Lake job to Sioux Falls architect Harold Spitznagel, but it certainly didn't sour him on South Dakota.

For information on the Badlands, call the National Park Service office at (605) 433-5361.

Heaven or hell?
SOUTH DAKOTA TOURISM

Die, Oh Honored Coyote

Few animals have been as simultaneously honored and reviled as the wily coyote. In South Dakota we revere him as the official state animal (so deigned by the state legislature, no less), but we also put a bounty on his head.

Coyote's PR problem didn't begin in South Dakota. Native American cultures of centuries ago believed a buzzard would not eat Coyote because the two are friends. Then along came Mark Twain who wrote, "He was not a pretty creature, or respectable either . . . The Coyote is a long, slim, sick and sorry looking skeleton, with a gray, wolfish skin stretched over it, a tolerably bushy tail that forever sags down with a despairing expression of forsakenness and misery, a furtive and evil eye, and a long sharp face, with slightly lifted lip and exposed teeth."

We blame the coyote for every dead calf on the prairie and every missing dog, cat, or chicken, whether or not we find a carcass. Yet, how many businesses are named in his honor? Who is mascot for the University of South Dakota in Vermillion? And, with the possible exception of the buffalo, is there another animal that better symbolizes the independent spirit of Dakotans?

When all is said and done, we suspect Chief Plenty Coups will be proved prophetic. He said, "The antelope have gone, the buffalo wallows are empty. Only the wail of the Coyote is heard."

★ ★

Our Nation's Exact Middle
Belle Fourche

Finding the exact center of anything as big as the United States of
America is tough—even very smart people in white lab coats at the
U.S. Department of Commerce and Environment's Science Services
Administration, Coast and Geodetic Services will attest to that.

Still, when they took their best shot at determining the exact center of the nation, the scientists agreed on a prairie spot about a half
hour's drive northwest of Belle Fourche. The nation's center was in
Kansas until 1959, when Alaska and Hawaii won statehood. That
shifted the center about 440 miles northward to a privately owned
ranch near Belle Fourche, a cowboy town of about 4,000 people
that has large rodeo sculptures by local artist Tony Chytka on its
street corners. City officials hope to eventually buy the land around
America's center point, but until that happens, you have to go over
or under a barbed wire fence.

To find the exact center, start at the junction of US 85 and US
212 in Belle Fourche and drive 13 miles north. Take a left on Harding
County Road and drive 7.8 miles until you see a gray barn on the left.
Look to your right for an orange post about 50 yards from the road.
Beware of rattlesnakes on warm days.

For more on the town and the center post, call (605) 892-2676 or
visit www.bellefourche.org.

Stone Johnnies and Journals
Belle Fourche

Travelers on the back roads of Butte and Harding Counties may
stumble upon piles of rocks that the local ranchers call "stone johnnies." As the story goes, the rocks were collected and erected by
bored sheepherders who had nothing more interesting to do as they
watched their flocks.

Archie Gilfillan, the veteran sheepherder from the 1930s who also
became a popular South Dakota author, said he and other herders

did a lot of reading. Some specialized in certain studies. For example, they might study chemistry "and try to find out what happens when you put some raisins and sugar and a little yeast in a jar of water and let them stand for a while," Gilfillan wrote in his book *Sheep*. Others, he noted, would study local history, particularly "the kind that never gets in the history books—or into any other books. Some take up the study of statistics, and get so they can predict probable increases in population—that is, among people they know."

Gilfillan compiled a long journal about the events and people of his West River sheep country. "Country people not only know all about each other, but they know the most intimate and hair-raising details . . . Many a man has believed that his family skeleton was safely locked in its closet, while in reality it was spending most of its time gallivanting around the country in a most unskeletonly manner."

Gilfillan's sheep wagon is now on display at the Dakota Discovery Museum in Mitchell; local families are hoping his journals remain locked away. Some wish Gilfillan had satisfied his boredom like the rest of the herders, by building more stone johnnies.

We can't show you Archie Gilfillan's journals, but there is a stone johnny sure to be found just off US 85 at mile marker 84, north of Belle Fourche.

Monument to a Bucking Bronc
Buffalo

If you like towns where they still talk about a horse that was born more than a century ago, then you'll adore Buffalo, where there are monuments and statues to a big bay known as Tipperary.

A colt was born on a ranch by Long Pines in 1905. He bolted from the corral the first time anyone tried to ride him, and after that he wasn't deemed fit for ranch work. The horse roamed the range until he was tried as a rodeo bronc. Ed Marty, the first to climb aboard, was promptly thrown to the street, whereupon he said, "It's a long, long way to Tipperary!" Thus, the horse got its name.

★ ★

Two champs—Yakima Canutt on Tipperary
SOUTH DAKOTA MAGAZINE

From 1915 to 1926 he bucked off ninety-one men. Only Yakima Canutt, a champion rider, stayed in the saddle during Tipperary's prime. The horse died during a blizzard in 1932. In 1955 local citizens erected a monument in Buffalo City Park, and in 2009 the town dedicated a half-size statue of the horse done by cowboy sculptor Tony Chytka. But memorials aren't necessary to keep Tipperary's legend alive in Harding County, South Dakota.

Photos and memorabilia of the great horse, plus an interesting saddle collection, are on display at the Buffalo Museum on US 85, which is open weekdays from 10:30 to 2:30 in the summer or by appointment (605-375-3800).

Our Oil Patch

"Black gold" is pumped from under the sagebrush and sandstone buttes of Harding County in extreme northwestern South Dakota. A few dozen wells have been scattered across the picturesque grasslands since oil was discovered here in 1954.

State wildlife experts watch the Oil Patch for spills, but the energy companies have few problems. One test of a cleanup is whether the native grasses grow back. They always do, a rancher told us, "and so do the weeds."

South Dakota's black gold lies in Harding County.

Russians Now Welcome
Cactus Flat

Remember the cold war when we worried that the Russians were coming? Public buildings had yellow and black "bomb shelter" signs, and families stocked their basements with rations. One South Dakota town even built a watchtower because its American Legion members figured they were under the likely Russian flight path, and they wanted to warn the Pentagon of any attack.

Few Americans realize that 150 missiles were buried in the West River prairie. The Minuteman IIs could travel 15,000 miles per hour and reach the Soviet Union in forty minutes. The Russians knew the missiles were there, however, so when the SALT treaty was signed in 1991, we agreed to remove them.

And we did—all but one. It lies near a little spot by the Badlands known as Cactus Flat. The National Park Service now gives tours of the missile site and its nearby contact station, where two soldiers sat 12 feet apart with keys that had to be turned simultaneously to activate the missile.

Only one missile was ever fired. A test done near Newell in March 1965 was proclaimed a success. The remaining missile is really only a simulation. You can view it through glass, and Russians spies are even welcome. We have nothing more to hide—or so we say.

For a tour of the missile site you must call ahead. Phone (605) 433-5552.

Smart Dogs (or Rats?)
Cactus Flat

The wise South Dakota prairie dog makes his way to the prairie dog town at Cactus Flat, by the east entrance to the Badlands. Tourists buy peanuts at the nearby Ranch Store (exit 131 along I-90) and feed them to the dogs, so they are both wise and fat. There are a few other peaceful places to be a prairie dog—some parks and preserves and zoos—but other than that, this is not a safe state. South Dakota cattlemen despise the little varmints because they destroy grasslands.

Hunters are allowed to shoot them year-round on private property, and during limited seasons on some public lands. It's not hard for sportsmen to get permission to hunt prairie dogs on private land or on the reservations. The state has even spread poison oats to control the population. But the Conata Basin in the Badlands is a safe haven.

A giant yellow and purple prairie dog
welcomes Badlands travelers.

Also at Cactus Flat is the world's only white prairie dog town. Local rancher Keith Crew rescued a few white prairie dogs during a widespread extermination program in the 1960s. Crew released them around Prairie Homestead, an authentic sod cabin and pioneer farm that he has preserved for tourists. The genes have spread, and now most of the dogs at Prairie Homestead are white.

Rancher Keith Crew kept a strain of white prairie dogs alive at his Prairie Homestead.

Some visitors also like to buy mounts of the dogs. Each generally costs about $100. The price, explained one taxidermist, is high because it's difficult to find a good specimen to mount. When shot, the little rodents often jump back in their holes before their demise. Consequently, the taxidermist must resort to flooding them out. Up to 1,000 gallons of water are sometimes needed to drown out a single prairie dog because their underground towns are so complex.

The famous explorers Lewis and Clark named the species. Local ranchers wish they'd have called them prairie rats, their true biological lineage. If so, the little critters probably wouldn't have such avid defenders. And the Ranch Store would sell a lot less peanuts.

Patrolled by Coyotes and Rattlers

Camp Crook

A Catholic priest and pilot started Sky Ranch as a home for troubled teenage boys on a 3,000-acre ranch south of Camp Crook, near the Little Missouri River. Rattlesnakes, coyotes, and mountain lions are the nearest neighbors.

Runaways are a problem at similar facilities, but seldom does a teen leave Sky Ranch. Most of them come from America's inner-city concrete jungles, unaccustomed to South Dakota's critters. A counselor once observed that when newcomers are told to watch for snakes and when they hear the howls of coyotes at night, "it's hard to get them to step off the concrete if you want them to."

Who needs fences when you're surrounded by varmints?

211

★ ★

Spurs, Stories, and Stuff
Dallas

Frank Day's Bar in the tiny town of Dallas has one of the West's biggest collections of historical cowboy hats and boots. Day started the collection and the bar in 1946. He gathered stories (including taped interviews with old cowboys) and also became the depository for memorabilia.

Arrowheads, hand-carved canes, guns, a bear coat worn by a freight hauler for Custer, spurs, bridles, and other collectibles hang from the walls and ceiling. The hats and boots belonged to famous rodeo cowboys, politicians, and other notables.

One of the many photos shows Tom McCrorey, a tough rancher who had a hole in the palm of his hand so big that you could see daylight through it. "He claimed a bear had mauled him," Day said, "but the bear must have had a revolver because the hole was perfectly round."

Frank Day died a few years ago, but his daughter Shelly has kept it all in the family. Ask for a reservation in these parts and they'll refer you to the nearest Indian tribe—but if you insist on calling ahead, the number is (605) 835-9866. The bar is along SD 18 on the outskirts of town.

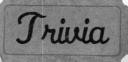

Trivia

The southern start of the 114-mile Mickelson Trail that runs through the Black Hills is in Edgemont. Bikers, hikers, and even horses are welcome—but a horse is required to carry a rider.

Horse Trap's Ancient Tree
Edgemont

South Dakota has some 200-year-old trees, and we also have some that are 200 million years old. One of the latter stands in the city park at Edgemont. The petrified tree was discovered at nearby Horse Trap Mountain and was moved to the park in 1926, where it serves as a curiosity for townspeople and visitors.

John McKnight stands by a tree that once was on his ranch.
JERRY WILSON

How does a tree become petrified? Only from the right sequence of wood, water, and mud. Scientists think the petrified trees of western South Dakota were part of a huge redwood forest some 200 million years ago. They were buried in water when the region became an inland sea about 60 to 80 million years ago. Then a volcanic explosion occurred, and a layer of ash settled over all the plants and animals. Those conditions eventually caused the wood to petrify in quartz crystals that are hard as steel, yet sometimes fragile enough to shatter.

Cannonball Lawn Decor
Faith

Pink flamingos, deer antlers, and wagon wheels are popular lawn ornaments in some South Dakota towns, but cannonballs are popular in Faith and certain other West River communities. These cannonballs are not the round missiles of the Revolutionary War, but something much older.

Eons ago, tiny rocks were formed when sedimentation attached to something like a leaf or walnut and began to grow. About sixty million years ago, the rocks were pushed into today's Dakotas by a glacier and deposited in a great sea. Time and water rounded the stones, and they've now become a popular decor for local home owners. Some people border their property with the stones, which are about the size of bowling balls. Others sit them on posts or create rock gardens.

Scientists refer to a geological region west of the Missouri River as the Cannonball Formation. There is a Cannonball River in North Dakota, and once upon a time there was a town called Cannonball in South Dakota, but it was flooded by the Oahe Dam project along with lots of the round rocks.

Many cannonballs have been picked up, but millions more lie beneath the loose soils of northwest South Dakota, especially in the scenic Grand and Moreau River valleys. Every year, a few more become exposed due to wind and rain.

Some South Dakota farmers and ranchers will give a visitor all the rocks and stones he wants to carry away, but you mustn't, of course, trespass on private property while searching for cannonballs. Furthermore, the cannonballs can be found in the very same habitat as rattlesnakes, so be careful if you receive permission.

Perhaps it would be safest to simply stroll the pleasant residential streets of Faith or travel north and visit Petrified Wood Park in Lemmon.

Cannonballs complement your pink flamingos.

Sacred Peace Pipe
Green Grass

According to the Lakota religion, the White Buffalo Calf Woman appeared before the Indians and gave them a pipe. "I have brought you this Buffalo Calf Leg Pipe so you can pray to God," she told them. "With this you will not starve, your children will grow, and your people will be healthy, and you will have life. Whenever you are in danger or in need of anything, you must respect this Pipe and pray with good intentions, and your prayers will be answered."

She entrusted the sacred pipe to one worthy person, and since then the pipe has been passed down through fourteen generations. Today the Keeper of the Pipe is Arvol Looking Horse. He lives in Green Grass, a tiny community on the Cheyenne River Indian Reservation. A Pipe Ceremony is held there annually, and a Pipe House was constructed in 1987.

A Barn-Size Thirst

Starting a town makes a man thirsty, and proof of that stands in the little town of Faith, where you'll find one of the West's few remaining wooden railroad icehouses. The barnlike structure was built in 1911—the year the town was formed—by a tavern owner named Flannery who used it for beer storage until Prohibition arrived in 1918. A copper floor on the second level held enough ice to cool the beer on the first level. The barn held three railcars full of beer. Today the icehouse is Faith's biggest museum exhibit.

No Truman Library for S.D.
Gregory

Tens of thousands of land-hungry men and women came to Tripp County in October 1911 for one of the West's last homestead lotteries. Among them was Harry Truman, who would become president of the United States three decades hence.

"I'll bet there'll be more bohunks and Rooshans up there than white men," he wrote to Bess, as he was en route. He rode a train packed with 686 other passengers. It was cold when they arrived, but Gregory had built a turreted Corn Palace and merchants were actively courting the hopefuls. Truman called it "a strictly modern town."

He paid $15, entered his lot, and left at 6 o'clock the next morning. His name was not drawn, so he did not get 160 acres. "Just keep imagining that my luck will change someday," he wrote to Bess.

And that's as close as Gregory has come to getting a presidential library.

Trivia

A lesser-known American celebrity did win the land lottery. Oscar Micheaux homesteaded east of Gregory before he found fame as America's first successful black filmmaker. He was also a fine novelist. Today Gregory celebrates its native son every August with the Oscar Micheaux Film Festival. For information on the festival, pheasant hunting, or other local activities, call (605) 835-8270 or visit www.cityofgregory.com.

★ ★

Mixing Bagels and Fry Bread
Kadoka

Bertha Martinsky wasn't the only single mother to try her luck
at homesteading in the Badlands. Most of the poor ladies soon
retreated from the desertlike landscape, but Mrs. Martinsky survived
by opening a general mercantile in nearby Kadoka.

Kadoka's historic preservation project

She tended the store every day but the Sabbath, when non-Jewish clerks took over. Locals called it the Jew Store, and the name stuck. The Lakota Indians were good customers, along with the local ranchers and the few farmers who survived in the Badlands.

Customers loved Mrs. Martinsky's doughnuts, which were a mix of Jewish bagels and Indian fry bread. They were selling for a dime a bag when she died in 1940 and the store closed.

Her descendants moved to nearby Rapid City and prospered. Little changed on Kadoka's main street, so the Jew Store was neither maintained nor destroyed. It stood empty, aging ungracefully, until Mrs. Martinsky's grandson, Rapid City philanthropist Stan Adelstein, decided to restore it for the town's centennial in 2006.

It's worth taking the Kadoka exit on I-90 to see a classic example of prairie historic preservation—and how it's contagious. As of this writing, several women are planning to restore the little town's hundred-year-old Pearl Hotel and turn it into a community gathering place.

America's Cheapest Magazine Publisher
Kadoka

If Paula Vogelgesang owned struggling magazines like *Time* or *Newsweek,* she'd buy only black ink, dismiss the entertainment editors, switch from glossy to newsprint, and probably invest the profits (yes, she'd show a profit) in more cows.

In an era when many of America's leading magazines have either folded or are failing financially, this rancher's wife from the tiny West River town of Wanblee (near Kadoka) has made a success of a quaint little publication called *Pennywise* that is full of ideas on how to live frugally and simply. Her mentors, she says, are the women who homesteaded in Jackson County and their daughters and granddaughters who survived the Great Depression, two world wars, and "lots of droughts."

Pennywise's Paula Vogelgesang

One issue advised readers that peroxide and dish soap absorbs skunk odor, that dish soap and chewing tobacco kills grasshoppers, and that shaving cream removes diesel smell from work clothes. Every issue has beef recipes, as might be expected from a magazine with a West River postmark, because this is the heart of the nation's cattle industry.

Readers supply many of the penny-pinching ideas. "JK" from Nebraska tells how to make household fertilizer from egg shells, and "AR" from Minnesota says lawn bags are perfect for keeping weeds out of flower beds. "TL" from Utah claims hot pepper sauce can loosen rusty nuts, and "CD" of Ohio cooks yellowed linens in water, milk, and soap to re-whiten them.

Vogelgesang is too cheap to use the magazine industry's direct-mail subscription model. Rather, she has learned that mothers-in-law will buy subscriptions for their spendthrift daughters-in-law as long as the magazine is sent anonymously. Mothers love their sons, so maybe that idea could have saved the now-defunct *Gourmet* magazine.

Interested in subscribing anonymously for your daughter-in-law—or even your wife? Visit www.smart-penny.com or call (605) 462-6495.

The Badlands Cross
Kadoka

When Brett Prang can't get a piece of steel welded, hammered, or cut just right, he's been known to run it over with his tractor.

Prang is a working rancher, and the cattle still come first. But a few years ago, he began to supplement ranch revenues with art sales—and with considerable success. He quickly established a reputation at regional art shows and galleries.

In the Badlands country south of Kadoka, where he and his wife, Tammy, run a 5,500-acre cattle ranch, he's best known for the

Brett Prang created a 38-foot metal
cross for the family cemetery.
JULI WILCOX

38-foot cross he erected in the family cemetery on Memorial Day of 2003. It stands over the graves of four generations who've ranched the same land.

The cross and other large sculptures by Prang are made of scrap tools and other ranch junk, like disc blades, ax heads, pulleys, levers, chains, and bolts. Prang made a 27-foot cross that can be purchased for $27,000, but he also makes smaller items that start at $5.

Tammy does leatherwork, including lampshades, mirrors, and bar stools. They have a studio on the ranch south of Kadoka. Just watch for the giant saguaro cactus along SD 73—the metal cactus, that is.

For more information on their art, call the Prangs at (605) 462-6373.

Ole's Petrified Park
Lemmon

If Lemmon's men hadn't been so hungry for a job in the 1930s, the city might not have a Petrified Wood Park today. Ole Quammen, an amateur geologist, had a vision of an outdoor museum that would show off the region's unusual stones and fossils. As the Great Depression worsened, federal money for public works projects became available, and Quammen suddenly had plenty of willing hands.

The men collected petrified wood, unusual stones, and spherical rocks known locally as "cannonballs." (See "Cannonball Lawn Decor" on page 214.) They hauled their finds to downtown Lemmon, and under Quammen's watchful eye, built cone-shaped trees, waterfalls, a castlelike museum, a wishing well, benches, and other oddities. The park is like nothing else—natural yet concocted, earthy yet moonlike.

Their creation is northwest South Dakota's biggest tourist attraction, and also one of the West's largest collections of geological and historical wonders. The stone works are unique, and the accompanying museum is also worth visiting. It features buffalo heads, livestock

Lemmon's lunar-looking Petrified Park

brands, a replicated bread wagon, and other memorabilia from Lemmon's ranching history.

Petrified Wood Park is at 500 Main Street in downtown Lemmon. Call (605) 374-3964 for information. Most visitors arrive in the summer months, but those who stop during the holiday season get a special treat: The cone-shaped cannonball trees are lighted for the occasion. That must have been Ole's idea.

Hay-Bale Humor

Don't call for an ambulance or hearse if you see legs stuck in a hay bale—most likely, it's a rancher's idea of a joke.

Hay-bale humor is alive and kicking in ranch country. We've seen those 1,000-pound rolls of hay gussied up like turkeys, strung together like gigantic centipedes, and painted like pumpkins.

Some funny folks in Kadoka have maintained a roadside rest stop made of a few hay bales, a toilet stool, and some recliners. The plumbing is poor and the privacy nil, but those minor inconveniences are more than overcome by a view of the Badlands and the excellent ventilation.

Baled and tied in Parkston

★ ★

Trivia

Lemmon, the northernmost town in South Dakota, was originally sited for North Dakota. But the founder, cattleman Ed "Boss Cowman" Lemmon, liked an occasional sip of whiskey, and when he realized that North Dakota was a dry state in 1907, he moved his town south to South Dakota. Visit www.lemmonsd.com or call (605) 374-5716 for information on Lemmon's paleontology and other activities, especially hunting and fishing.

Stone Borders Make Good Neighbors
Ludlow

Only two states in the nation share a border fully and permanently distinguished by quartzite markers. Weighing about 800 pounds each, they were installed between North Dakota and South Dakota a few years after Congress divided Dakota Territory in 1889.

Surveyor Charles Bates was in charge of the project. He joked that he should be eligible for admission into the Humane Society because he had erected 720 of the best scratching posts ever made for cattle.

Since their laborious installation, many of the pink posts have been lost to thieves, buried by dust storms, or removed for road construction. But some still divide the Dakotas a century later.

The story is told of a road construction engineer who couldn't find any of the boundary markers, so he resurveyed a stretch of the border. When he finished, he went to a nearby farmhouse and told the farmer that he had interesting news. "You don't live in North Dakota after all," said the engineer. "According to my survey, you live in South Dakota." "Thank the Lord," replied the farmer. "I don't know if I could stand another winter in North Dakota!"

Want to find a marker? As noted, many are missing, but you might get lucky if you check north–south border roads. We found the westernmost stone in a remote field north of Ludlow. It marks the tri-state corner of Montana and the two Dakotas; the year 1892 and other data are etched in the purple granite. To get there, you'll need to ask a local expert for directions. Ours read like this: "Turn at the snow-plow blade and go past where there used to be a gate (you'll see the post). Follow the fence line. Marker is below the hill. Good luck."

The author, by the stone boundary marker at the tri-state corner of the Dakotas and Montana.
BILL JOHNSON

★ ★

Cowboy Country Spa
Midland

Not many West River ranching towns can boast of having a spa on
Main Street, but people have been soaking in Midland (population
170) since 1939 at the Stroppel Hotel. The cowboys' spa is a century-
old wood-frame hotel that was moved across the railroad tracks in
1907, blocking train traffic for several hours. A picture of the momen-
tous occasion is humorously titled "A Holdup on the Northwestern."

John Stroppel suffered from pneumonia as a child, and found
relief from soaking in the hot spring water that runs through the
area. Convinced of its therapeutic value, he bought the hotel in
1939 and drilled wells to supply the baths with the warm water (119
degrees). In the early years clients stayed for three weeks. Stroppel
believed that the human body recycles its blood cells every twenty-
one days, and soaking in the baths for that same time period could
rejuvenate your health.

When George Stroppel took over the family business, he studied
massage therapy and added it as a treatment. The hotel (602 Main)
now operates as a bed-and-breakfast. Call (605) 843-2802 or check
www.stroppelinn.com.

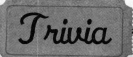
Trivia

While traveling south-central South Dakota near the Rosebud Reservation, tune your radio dial to 96.1 FM to enjoy an entirely new
listening experience. Indian-operated KINI Radio interjects traditional
Lakota music with modern rock, local weather, and tribal news. Farther west you'll catch KINI's twin station, KILI, at 90.1 FM by the Pine
Ridge Reservation.

* *

A Showman for Motor Heads
Murdo

The King's '76 Harley is parked here. And you've heard of the Model A and Model T, but have you ever seen a Model N? Or a '31 Pierce Arrow, or an entire shop full of Mustangs?

The Pioneer Auto Show has all that and more in forty buildings stuffed with nostalgia. The cars and motorcycles alone are worth the price of admission, but Dave Geisler, the longtime proprietor and chief host, has also collected railroad memorabilia, rock and mineral exhibits, antique toys and games, pioneer storefronts, farm machinery (including the world's fastest manure spreader), and hours worth of other things to see in one of the world's biggest private auto collections.

While we were there, a Utah visitor told Geisler that he saw two cars in the Murdo museum worth $750,000 or more. Dave walked away with a big grin and said, "I get to meet more motor heads!"

A hot-rod manure spreader at Murdo
PIONEER AUTO SHOW

★ ★

Geisler loves to entertain. He pops nickels in antique jukeboxes, shows kids a furry monster locked away in a box trap, and starts a player piano that plunks honky-tonk tunes. He probably could have made a fortune running a basketball booth in a traveling carnival. But his family heritage is cars, and you can't truck hundreds of them from town to town, so people come to him.

The Pioneer Auto Show is located at exit 192 on I-90. Visit online at www.pioneerautoshow.com or call (605) 669-2691.

Devil, Beware of Barns
Murdo

Not many South Dakota farmers build round barns, but keep your eyes peeled and you'll see a few in your travels. *South Dakota Magazine* counted three dozen in the 1990s.

Easy-to-find favorites in West River country include the Butte County fairgrounds pavilion at Nisland, a Pennington County fairgrounds barn in Rapid City that was once an Alfalfa Palace, a unique vertical-log round barn just south of the Black Hills National Cemetery near Sturgis, and—grandest of all—the main building at 1880 Town, 23 miles west of Murdo at exit 170 on I-90. The fourteen-sided structure's intricate wooden rafters are an architectural wonder.

Some farmers built round because they felt the circular structure was strong. Others liked it because they could drop hay through a hole in the center of the loft while the cattle or sheep stood with their heads to the center and their tails to the outside—thus the feed moved from the center of the barn, through the animal, and exited near the barn door.

Historians believe some early American farmers also liked round barns because they thought they were a deterrent to the devil, who supposedly likes to hide in square corners. No corners, no devil? If being good was only that easy.

For information on 1880 Town and its big round barn, visit www.1880town.com or call (605) 344-2236.

The big round barn at 1880 Town

★ ★

The Sheep Capital
Newell

Cattle for respect—sheep to pay the bills!
—*West River axiom*

Don't let anyone pull the wool over your eyes—Newell is the Sheep Capital of the United States. As far as we can tell, the Butte County town wins by default. That's unusual in farm country, where a dozen towns call themselves the Hay Capital, and others simultaneously claim corn, hogs, and sundry other commodity honors.

West River is sheep country.

★ ★

Trivia

Fans of the film *Dances with Wolves* will enjoy the movie memorabilia at 1880 Town in Murdo. It has the freight wagons and other props from the film, including the horse Buck, corralled out back.

Visit Newell any day but Thursday and you might wonder why it deserves such prominence. There won't be a sheep to be shorn, or even seen. But on Thursdays ranchers from five states haul their ewes and lambs to market here. The sheep growers speak English, but sometimes it sounds like a different dialect as they talk of broken mouths, bum lambs, short-term ewes, killer bucks, and unshorns. The best place to learn "Sheepish" is at the Newell auction barn. The nation's very best sheep have flocked here every September for the past sixty-two years to compete in the Annual Newell Ram Show.

For more on the sheep show, visit www.cityofnewell.com or call (605) 456-1010. Newell is easy to find; it's a two-hour drive northwest of South Dakota's *Baa*-dlands.

A Treasure Cave on the Rez
Pine Ridge

The Pine Ridge Reservation is 1.7 million acres of steep hills and valleys, cliffs, mesas, and pine forests. And according to one of America's biggest and best-known cattlemen, it also has a cave filled with relics and treasures.

Ed Lemmon, aka Boss Cowman, was a bigger-than-life cowboy who started as a Texas trail driver and ended up with more cattle and more land than anyone. They say he still holds the world record for roping and delivering 900 calves to the branders in a single day. He knew every valley in western South Dakota, and most in Montana, Nebraska, and Wyoming.

Lemmon was searching for lost cattle in the White River valley of the Pine Ridge Reservation when he rode onto a cave opening and decided to explore. With a torch in one hand and his revolver in the other, he walked deep into the cave and came upon what he called a treasure room. Many years later he wrote, "The walls were covered with hangings and with other relics of all kinds. I didn't see any white robes there, but there were lots of others. I just stood there and gazed as far as I could see in the light of my torch. It was about all the same for 40 or 50 feet, to where the cave widened to about 25 feet across by 15 or 20 feet high, and all of it was covered with relics."

Figuring it was a bandit's hideout, he departed quickly. Later that same year, Lemmon returned to look for the cave but could not find the opening.

"The Rez," as Pine Ridge is called by the Oglala Lakota who live there, is the second-largest reservation in the United States. If Boss Cowman couldn't find the cave a second time, you aren't likely to have any luck either, so leave your flashlight at home.

South Dakota Discovered in South Dakota
Quinn

The last of the dinosaurs died when an asteroid hit Earth sixty-five million years ago. They had no warning, but take comfort: Smart people with very big telescopes are now watching for signs of the next big collision, and one of them is on duty in the tiny Badlands town of Quinn.

Ron Dyvig set up his equipment in an old hospital in 1998, and within a few years he was rated thirtieth among 263 observatories worldwide. He has discovered several dozen asteroids, and in one instance he was given the honor of naming a 2-mile-wide chunk of space. He decided to call it South Dakota.

* *

You won't want to visit the other South Dakota because it's a few hundred million miles away, and it's probably rougher and drier than its namesake's Badlands.

Let's hope the two Dakotas never collide, because even an asteroid the size of a football field would wipe out a city. Think of the damage South Dakota would cause if it ever hit Earth.

Ron Dyvig, by his high-rated observatory
JERRY WILSON

Wacipi Etiquette

Eight percent of South Dakotans are Native Americans, meaning their ancestry predates Columbus, the Pilgrims, and all the other immigrants who make up our country.

Our Native people live in towns and cities across the state. However, the vast majority live on nine Indian reservations, and all nine welcome visitors. Many of the Lakota (West River) and Dakota (East River) Indians are skilled artisans. You'll find their arts and crafts (including the famed star quilts) in shops on the reservations and across the state.

Powwows provide a good opportunity to visit a reservation. *Wacipis* (pronounced *wa-cheep-ees*) are open to the public. Some are well-organized competitive events, while others may be very informal and loosely organized. They are social, cultural, and sacred in nature. Here are a few etiquette tips to observe, whether you are at a powwow or anywhere in Indian Country:

Questions—We all like to have visitors show interest in our culture, but don't go overboard. At some point you might appear nosy.

Dress—Powwow is a sacred ceremony. Don't dress formally, but show proper respect; no halter tops, bare feet, or mini-shorts.

Alcohol—Several reservations are "dry," meaning no alcoholic beverages are for sale, so guests shouldn't bring coolers. Obviously, drugs and firearms are also off-limits.

Pay attention—Every powwow has a master of ceremonies. The activities may seem quite informal, but please listen; he may be asking for silence or directing you to stand for the flag ceremony.

You can dance—Most powwows include an intertribal dance that is open to everyone, and that means you. Again, be respectful. This is no time for the Twist.

Bring a chair—and a blanket. The accommodations may be quite humble, so be prepared to make yourself comfortable. Don't sit in the front of the circle because that may be reserved for dancers.

Photographs—Most dancers don't mind if you take pictures with the same courtesy that you would show at your cousin's church wedding. But it never hurts to ask.

Patriotism—Native Americans are very respectful of the same U.S. government that forced them from their lands just a few generations ago. They are always quick to join the military when the United States goes to war, and their patriotism shows at pow-wows—so be prepared to stand and remove head coverings when the American and tribal flags are presented.

You can join the dancing.
SOUTH DAKOTA TOURISM

Visit the tribes' joint tourism site at www.attatribal.com or the state's visitor site, www.travelsd.com, for powwow schedules.

Also on "the Rez"

Visit the Red Cloud Heritage Center, an art exhibit and museum just west of Pine Ridge in a historic mission. Native American artists bring their work from many miles around for advice and marketing assistance. Call (605) 867-5491.

Hang out at Big Bat's, a big, busy convenience store that acts as a small mall for the Pine Ridge people, who don't have many other shops and stores available. On some days the Lakota-owned store has an international atmosphere due to the people from around the world who come to learn about the Lakota culture. Big Bat's is like no other quick-stop in South Dakota. The store is in the center of Pine Ridge, at the intersection of SD 18 and SD 87.

Higher Ground, one of Indian country's classiest coffee shops, serves baked goods and lattes just a block to the east of Big Bat's. Cedar Pass Lodge, a tribally owned gift shop (605-433-5460), has been operating on the east edge of the Badlands since 1928. You'll find it at 20681 SD 240.

The Pine Ridge Reservation stretches from the Badlands to the Nebraska border. Visit www.oglalasiouxtribe.com for more information about things to do and see on "the Rez."

Leave a Mark
Reliance

For one green dollar you can leave your mark in Lyman County. Thousands of people have done it. The dollars, with messages scribbled on them, are taped and pinned all over the walls of the Reliance Bar.

Nobody remembers how the custom began, but after all these years the faded cash is a cultural composite of the town of 160 people. The bills memorialize deceased relatives, celebrate birthdays and

★ ★

Trivia

On Wednesdays in the summer, Reliance Bar proprietor Denny Marsh serves burgers and steaks from a charcoal grill. If you stay after dark, keep an eye peeled for the bar's ghost. He is always sighted in a trench coat, hat, and vest. We also know that he's short and he's no thief—he never disturbs the dollars on the wall.

anniversaries, and proclaim loves. Soldiers, hunters, dignitaries, and tourists leave some. Foreigners have signed paper currency from their homelands; several bills bear the names of South African laborers who came to Lyman County to help with the wheat harvest. A Native American artist folded his dollar to look like a buffalo head.

It is only natural to want to leave a mark. Dogs do it on fire hydrants. Cavemen scratched drawings on soft rocks. Rich men commission sculptures. In the end most of us want a gravestone. Posting a dollar in the Reliance Bar (101 Main Street) is less pretentious than those customs. But if you want to stand out, write your name on a Ben Franklin and tape it up.

Call (605) 473-0130 for more information.

The Creston Dinosaur
Scenic

What's that concrete dinosaur doing down along the Cheyenne River? Even the local people probably wonder today. We had to find some true old-timers before we learned that Ed Burgess and Bud Murphy, who owned the little town of Creston that once stood across the road, built the dinosaur. They hoped it might cause travelers to slow down just enough to notice the Creston Store.

It obviously failed as a marketing gimmick, because the dinosaur outlasted the town. The T. rex replica is still well cared for, however, and can be seen just east of the Cheyenne River off SD 44 between Rapid City and Scenic.

Of course, similar dinosaurs stand on a hill overlooking Rapid City, and another Jurassic cousin welcomes visitors to Wall on the north

The dinosaur outlived the town.
SOUTH DAKOTA MAGAZINE

end of the Badlands. Those dinosaurs are in relatively citified surroundings, obviously planted to get your attention. The Creston Dinosaur, however, stands all by his lonesome self in the river valley.

Where Hugh Glass Fought Lord Grizzly
Shadehill Reservoir

One of America's greatest survival stories began at a spot that now lies beneath Shadehill Reservoir near Lemmon. Today Shadehill is a refreshing spot of blue on the big, brown landscape of Perkins County. Long before the reservoir was created, grizzly bears were the king of the food chain. Native Americans and early explorers told many tales of encounters with grizzlies, but none compare with the Hugh Glass adventure.

Glass was a sailor who was captured by pirates and had to join them or walk the plank. He jumped ship off the coast of Texas, swam to shore, and walked to Kansas, where the Pawnees held him for years. Finally, he escaped and headed up the Missouri River as a trapper in the 1830s.

Among mountain men Glass was regarded as someone to be depended on—which only magnified the crime he suffered at the hands of "friends." He was attacked and mauled by a grizzly and then left to die by companions who feared an Indian attack. Worst of all, they broke the mountain man's sacred code, taking his "possibles sack," rifle, powder horn, bullets, and blanket.

Too tough to die, Glass regained consciousness and crawled almost 200 miles across rugged country to Fort Kiowa, near present-day Chamberlain. He lived on berries, ants, mice, and a thirst for revenge. But after reaching civilization, he eventually forgave his companions.

Movies and books (Frederick Manfred's *Lord Grizzly* being the best) have told his story, but unless you go to Shadehill Reservoir and crawl on your belly for a few yards, you can't even begin to imagine his amazing ordeal.

The West River Cattle Run

"The difference between a cowboy and a rancher is this: The cowboy has a big buckle that covers his belly; the rancher has a big belly that covers his buckle."

—Overheard at St. Onge Livestock

South Dakota has 750,000 people and 1,800,000 momma cows. No, we don't each own 2.4 cows. They are concentrated in herds of a few dozen to a few hundred. The big herds are in West River, where most of the land is too rough and fragile for anything but grass and livestock.

Almost every cow has a calf in the spring, so in autumn lots of 500-pound bawling babies are sold at cattle livestock auctions. Buyers and sellers call it the Cattle Run, and it's a fascinating piece of Americana.

A livestock auction barn is the gathering place. Cattle-sale day is a Rotary Club lunch, the bank board meeting, golf at the country club, and Thanksgiving—all at once. Add a dash of Wall Street or the Chicago Mercantile, overshoes, and kerchiefs, and you get the picture. This is business with some socialization. Some might call it networking, but nobody's promoting anything except beef.

When ranchers bring their calves to town, the whole family goes along. Sometimes three generations sit on the wood bleachers and wait their herd's turn with the auctioneer and buyers. Hired hands also come. The rancher usually buys supper for all after the sale. A celebration is expected, because the cowman usually gets just one respectable check a year.

Some of the best and biggest cattle auctions happen right along I-90, the east–west road you're most apt to travel across South Dakota. Feel free to stop at Fort Pierre and St. Onge (Friday sales),

Presho (Thursdays), Philip (Tuesdays), and Faith (Mondays). Other livestock barns are spread across South Dakota.

Although the big Cattle Run is generally in October and November, smaller sales occur throughout the year. Just one tip: If you visit a sale barn with a restaurant, please don't ask for fish or chicken. That's like ordering a T-bone at Fisherman's Wharf in San Francisco.

Cowboys visit by the corrals at St. Onge Livestock.
SOUTH DAKOTA MAGAZINE

★ ★

An Arthritis Cure?

Pete Lemley, a colorful rancher who lived next to the Creston Dinosaur, suffered from arthritis in his old age. One day, while he was shutting a gate, a bumblebee stung his arthritic knuckles. They swelled for a day, but in the morning the swelling was down and the arthritis was gone.

Convinced that the bee venom had cured him, Pete scraped the flesh on his arm and applied bee's venom over a two-month period. He never complained about arthritis again, according to his daughter, Maggie Warren, in her book titled *The Badlands Fox.*

Why Use a Rooster When You Have a Cessna?
Shadehill Reservoir

The world's biggest wind vane sways high in the Perkins County sky, about 12 miles south of Lemmon near Shadehill Reservoir. Frank Rosenau and his son, Joel, used a crane to lift a Cessna 310 atop an old radar tower. A steady breeze points the plane windward and even twirls its propellers.

Rosenau admits there's no practical application for the wind vane except to entertain travelers along SD 73. The popular Shadehill Reservoir and its adjacent recreation area is just a half mile from the 45-foot-high Cessna.

The Rosenaus collect and sell all sorts of oddities—like cranes, Russian tank engines, a Caterpillar (how many uses does the average person have for one of those?), and military surplus items such as chloride by the barrel. One thing they don't have is a traditional rooster wind vane. Fortunately, they had an extra airplane.

244

Which way is the Cessna blowing?
SOUTH DAKOTA MAGAZINE

* *

A Town Built by Billboards
Wall

Wall Drug is one of America's favorite small-business success stories. Ted and Dorothy Hustead were struggling to keep their little drug-store alive in the Badlands during the 1930s when Dorothy came upon the idea of offering free ice water to thirsty motorists heading for the Black Hills.

Dorothy, who'd taught literature in Sioux Falls, wrote some cute signs:

GET A SODA
GET ROOT BEER
TURN NEXT CORNER
JUST AS NEAR
TO HIGHWAY 16 & 14
FREE ICE WATER

WALL DRUG

Ted joked that it was hardly Wordsworth, but he and a local teenager posted the signs. Before they returned from the highway, the first customers had already arrived. The rest is history. Over two million people a year now stop at Wall Drug Store, the world's most famous pharmacy.

Trivia

Some of Wall Drug's attractions are kitschy, but many are very unique. For example, the Husteads always supported Western and Native American artists. Through the years they acquired paintings by Harvey Dunn, N. C. Wyeth, Harold Von Schmidt, and Frank McCarthy, among many others. The paintings hang on the restaurant walls for all to enjoy.

Wall Drug is South Dakota's favorite store.
SOUTH DAKOTA TOURISM

Ted and son Bill erected billboards of all sizes in a five-state area until Lady Bird Johnson's highway beautification program outlawed most of them. As you drive across South Dakota, you'll notice that not only can you fight city hall, but you can even fight the feds—billboards are still popular here, largely because the Husteads actively lobbied to protect them. Recently, lawmakers in Pierre were debating the aesthetics of 150-foot-tall wind turbine towers when one remarked, "I don't mind how they look as long as they don't obstruct our billboards."

The Hustead family has had help spreading the signs. Soldiers plastered them all over Europe during World War II, and the same thing happened in Korea, Vietnam, and both Gulf War conflicts. Every customer is offered a free sign, and many take them home and hang them on barns, garages, and fences.

The Husteads soon learned to not only quench their visitors' thirsts, but also to entertain. Through the years they created one of the most popular roadside attractions in the USA. Bill came into the family business in 1951 and expanded the store to 76,000 square feet.

Wall Drug (510 Main Street) continues to change, but it still has all the old favorites—buffalo burgers, a bucking horse, nickel coffee, and big chocolate doughnuts. Today Bill's sons, Rick and Teddy, run it. And, yes, ice water is the same price.

For details call (605) 279-2175 or visit www.walldrug.com.

Frank Leahy's Debut

Winner

> Prayers work better when players are bigger.
>
> *—Notre Dame Coach Frank Leahy*

A sign over Winner's outdoor sports stadium proclaims it to be Frank Leahy Bowl, named for the legendary Notre Dame football coach who was raised here. It was in Winner where he developed an early reputation as a schemer.

The Leahy legend began in 1922 when Winner was losing to rival Gregory 108–0. Just when it seemed the game could get no worse, the ref blew his whistle and mysteriously ejected a baffled Winner starter. "What did I do wrong?" he asked. The Winner coach had no alternative but to replace the starter with an untested eighth-grader named Frank Leahy.

Young Frank didn't turn the game around, but he left the field with a huge grin. After sitting on the bench all season, he'd finally found a way into a game. Years later the truth surfaced: The referee was dating Leahy's sister, and Frank had convinced him beforehand that if the score was lopsided, it wouldn't matter if someone got ejected.

Leahy often credited his South Dakota upbringing for his win-at-any-cost attitude. He said ranchers might bet land or livestock on the outcome of Winner's football and baseball games, so he learned as a teenager that sloppy play could cost a man dearly and put your position in jeopardy.

★ ★

On many Sunday afternoons during the summer, Winner's county museum staff serves homemade ice cream or other treats at a huge wooden horseshoe-shaped counter that came from the historic Joe's Cafe in the museum's main building along SD 18.

Thus it's fair to ask: Did Winner's leaders name the stadium in his honor because of his 87-11-9 coaching record at Notre Dame—or was it payback for the cows he helped them win?

The Big Foot Ride

Wounded Knee

A horseback ride across the length of South Dakota has become a December tradition. The Big Foot Memorial Ride retraces the trail of Chief Big Foot and the Sioux Indians who followed him from the Standing Rock Reservation in northern South Dakota to Wounded Knee, a tiny but historic village near the southern border of the state.

Wounded Knee is a town name synonymous with sadness. It was there that the Seventh Cavalry killed 300 Indians and left many more freezing and injured in the Badlands snow.

The Big Foot Memorial Ride honors not only those who were lost, but also today's youths and future leaders of the Lakota. In recent years the annual ride—which is often met with bone-chilling cold and wind—has also served as a way to honor and remember loved ones who are serving the United States in the military overseas.

Visitors to Wounded Knee today will see a hilltop cemetery with a mass grave for the 1890 victims, along with other grave markers. A modest visitor center (605-867-2228) below the hill has exhibits of the massacre and of a second series of confrontations that occurred in 1973.

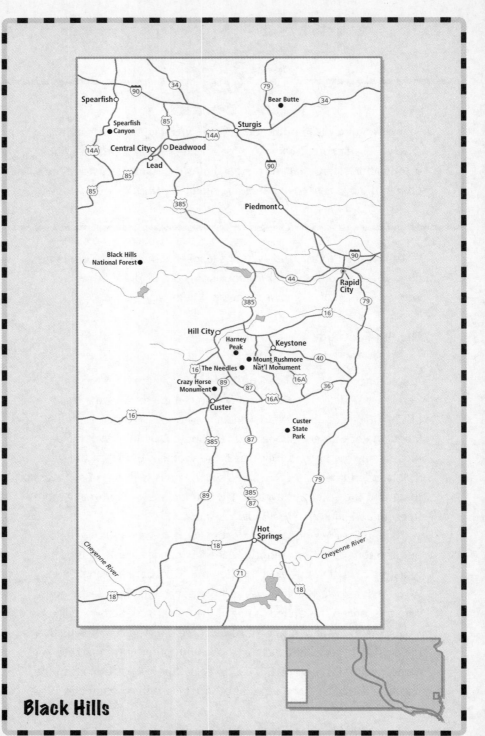

Black Hills

5

Black Hills

The mountain dwellers of the Black Hills are taller than prairie South Dakotans. Generally, they have darker hair, stubbier noses, and hazel eyes—and if you believe any of that, then you'll be a sucker for jacka-lopes, fool's gold, concrete dinosaurs, and all the other malarkey that adds flavor to our Black Hills culture.

Seriously, many of our mountain folk are fair-haired Scandinavians who grew up on East River farms or flatland cities and migrated to higher ground. Who can blame them? Where better to enjoy picturesque vil-lages in deep valleys, separated by ridge upon ridge of pine and spruce trees that take on hues of black and blue as they stretch to the horizon?

For all their height and expanse, these mountains are accessible to man. They've been mined, farmed, forested, hunted, skied, and hiked. Logging trails and mining roads circle many of them, especially in the northern woods.

Despite man's efforts to tame them, the mountains still appear wild, rugged, and free. While most of the big mines have closed, solitary gold diggers attack the slopes with picks and shovels, hoping to find the big vein.

Tourists fill the Black Hills towns and roads in summer, but the mountains become quiet refuges for those tall, dark mountain natives—and visitors tough enough to endure the crisp, clear mountain air. Whatever season you go, this chapter offers some travel pointers.

★ ★

A Shot-up Saloon
Central City

Before Johnny Daniels died in 1982, he made Wyola Ogren promise she wouldn't change his beloved saloon in Central City, so bullet holes are still clearly visible in the woodwork, and two golden eagles roost close to the ceiling.

Ogren continues to run the place. She says the bullet holes were courtesy of Daniels, who kept a gun under the bar and occasionally fired over the heads of rowdy customers to get their attention. Nobody remembers when the mounted eagles arrived, but it was before they were a protected species—everyone is certain of that.

Few businesses remain in the Lawrence County town that lies midway between Lead and Deadwood (thus its name), but it's always had a saloon. The town was founded shortly after the gold rush of 1876, and it boasted more than 4,000 citizens before floods and fires knocked it down to size. Today less than 200 live there.

The first saloon was called the Shoofly. Soon, the popular drinking spot was the Blue Diamond, run in the century-old building where Daniels presided for decades. Called the Silver Dollar during his tenure, he attached silver coins to the wood bar until the 1970s, when silver prices jumped and he decided they were too tempting to patrons.

Ogren now calls it the Casino Bar. Old rifles and shotguns hang behind the bar, near the eagles and the bullet holes. Stop by at 136 Main Street or call ahead, (605) 578-1824.

Custer: Buzzard or Angel?
Custer

A million people a year pass through the scenic little city called Custer, the oldest community in the Black Hills. Most are oblivious to the controversy that was started when the town's namesake, Lieutenant Colonel George Armstrong Custer, arrived in 1874 on a reconnaissance mission.

Custer came to investigate rumors of gold mining in the Black Hills. He was supposedly assigned to keep miners and settlers out of the mountains, which belonged to Native Americans by virtue of the Fort Laramie Treaty.

However, Custer entered the Black Hills with a thousand well-armed soldiers, armed with Gatling guns and a 3-inch cannon. It seemed like a lot of artillery, if the mission was to scare off miners

Lloyd and Webster Kreitz, with Lloyd's sculpture of Custer
SOUTH DAKOTA MAGAZINE

and farmers. Historians still wonder whether he came to keep the peace or to start an Indian war. Therein lies the controversy.

Near the town's main street stands a pale blue 14-foot-tall statue of Custer with wings, created by local sculptor Lloyd Kreitz. Both buzzards and angels wear wings. Kreitz, with a sly grin, says he leaves it to you to decide the meaning.

For a more open dialogue, keep your eyes peeled for a real man who looks a lot like Custer. That'll be Mitch McLain, a local historian who dresses the part of Custer in the summer months and makes himself available for anything from a photo-op to a serious discussion of whether the military's "golden boy" was a provocateur or peacemaker.

Bring a Knife and Some Nickels
Custer

Even real ranches don't always have cowhands that move—especially on hot days—but stick a wooden nickel in the elaborate ranch scene at the National Museum of Woodcarving and things happen: The windmill pumps water, horses wag their tails, and, yes, even the laziest cowboy gets busy.

The museum was created to showcase the work of Dr. Harley Niblack, a trailblazing Colorado chiropractor who invented a weight-loss machine and a technique to heat and heal tissue. In his forties he became one of America's great woodcarvers, working up to twenty hours some days and using dental tools to attain great detail. The museum's Wooden Nickel Theater is an exhibit of the doc's animated scenes.

Three of Niblack's works were on loan to the Smithsonian before the Schaffer family opened the National Museum of Woodcarving in Custer to give his life's work a home. Works by other great woodcarvers, including caricature carvers, are also on display, and more than thirty scenes by an original Disneyland animator can be viewed. Resident carvers are often in the studio, practicing their techniques.

The museum is open May through October on US 16 West.

Call (605) 673-4404 for more information or visit www.blackhills .com/woodcarving. Bring your knife and take a class.

Where's the End of Jewel Cave?
Custer

Few frontiers remain in North America, but explorers are still searching for the end of Jewel Cave in the southern Black Hills. Scientists have traveled passages extending 135 miles, and they have no reason to think they are near the end. That makes Jewel Cave, west of Custer, the world's second longest.

Cave exploration isn't for everybody. The temperature is a humid forty-nine degrees. Sometimes you must proceed on your belly. And, of course, it's very dark. Fortunately, the National Park Service arranges comfortable tours—some even by elevator—to scenic chambers where visitors get an interior look at the sixty-million-year-old Black Hills.

So where does the cave end? Will a Jewel Cave spelunker someday step into the sunshine and see a red Nebraska Cornhusker banner on the nearest mailbox? Scientists say we probably won't know in our lifetimes.

South Dakotans figure there are two benefits: One is the mystique of having a cave without an end, and the other is a savings in exit signs.

You'll find the cave's entrance 13 miles west of Custer at 11149 US 16 (phone 605-673-2288).

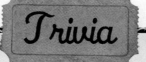

Trivia

Custer lies in a beautiful valley surrounded by forested peaks. Call the chamber of commerce at (800) 992-9818 or visit www .custersd.com for information on activities and accommodations.

Naming Your Gold Mine

Gold mining is a rare but respected occupation in the Black Hills. You can still file for a claim, which gives you permission to dig or pan on about twenty acres in the Black Hills National Forest. Of course, most of the easy spots are taken. Try not to be a claim jumper, though sometimes it's hard to find your exact coordinates in the backwoods—especially if you see a big nugget soaking in a creek. Call the Black Hills National Forest (605-673-9200) for maps and details.

Once you file a claim, you'll want to name your mine. Historically, mines have been named for famous characters, interesting geography, intriguing women, or heartfelt feelings. You might find inspiration in these all-time favorite names:

- Holy Terror Mine, named after the miner's wife

- Homestake, derived from the miners' hopes of getting a stake to buy a home

- Balky Mule Mine, on Jim Creek in Pennington County, for an obvious reason

- Bengal Tiger Mine, northwest of Hill City, for black and yellow streaks of ore

- Black Nell Mine, in honor of a madam from Deadwood

- Yankee Boy Mine in Lawrence County, named by William Fagen for his favorite chewing tobacco

- Antietam Mine, claimed by David Ellis, who fought in the Civil War's famous Battle of Antietam

✭ ✭

Who's Herding Whom?
Custer State Park

Black Hills cowboys say you can herd a buffalo anywhere he wants
to go. They ought to know. On the first weekend of every October,
some of the best in the West help Custer State Park officials gather
all of the buffalo and herd them into corrals.

The roundup begins with a short prayer, offered for the safety
of the riders, horses, and buffalo. Then the dust flies. The ground

The buffalo roundup is a rite of autumn in the Southern Hills.
SOUTH DAKOTA TOURISM

257

★ ★

trembles and shakes from the thundering hooves of 1,500 buffalo. Old bulls weigh up to two tons, and in autumn they'd prefer to be left alone, so they can get surly and stubborn.

However, nobody gets hurt. Park workers erect fences to help guide the herd into the corrals, and a few ATVs and pickups are also on hand to provide backup to the riders. These days, it's more show than work. When the dust settles, everyone gathers for an arts festival, chili cook-off, and other pleasantries while the buffalo are sorted, vaccinated, and readied for winter.

Want to buy your very own buffalo? Then return about seven weeks later (usually the third Saturday of November), when about a third of the herd is sold at public auction. Prices range from a few hundred dollars for a calf to a few thousand for the best cows and bulls. Set some money aside for fencing—you'll need it.

The park's Web site is www.custerstatepark.info; phone (605) 255-4515.

The Sound of the American West
Custer State Park

Some naturalists call the coyote's howl the symbolic sound of the West, but those folks probably aren't residents of the Black Hills. Natives here prefer the musical bugle of the bull elk in autumn.

The bull attracts mates with his powerful call. When a thousand-pound animal proclaims to all females within earshot that he owns the mountain, it is worth hearing.

Some humans summon bulls with an elk call that mimics the mating call. However, you don't want to be too good at cow talk: Males are known to get a little crazy.

Elk roam much of the Black Hills and some Indian reservations in South Dakota, but the best place to hear or see them is Custer State Park in the Southern Hills.

Hold on to Your Hat!

Wind Cave, south of Custer, was officially "discovered" in 1881 by Tom and Jesse Bingham. While hunting they felt a sudden, strong breeze that blew off their hats: It was air escaping from the underground tunnel. However, outlaws used the cave as a hideout before that, and according to Sioux history, it was where White Buffalo Calf Woman delivered the sacred peace pipe to the Lakotas.

Wind Cave is a sacred Sioux landmark.

Crazy Man's Jewelry

Indian wise man Black Elk once described gold as "a yellow metal that makes *Wasichus* [white men] crazy."

Crazy is right. White men scrambled like ants in a disturbed anthill when gold was discovered in the Black Hills in 1876. One of the miners was Henri LeBeau. Legend has it that the Frenchman was resting under a Black Hills tree, dreaming of his homeland, when he conjured up the grapevine design that has become the standard of Black Hills jewelry makers. He opened a goldsmith shop and did quite well.

LeBeau's design showed up in other mining camps, but it came to be known as Black Hills Gold no matter where it was made. All fakery came to an abrupt stop in 1981 when our mountain jewelers—normally bitter rivals—banded together and persuaded a federal

Landstrom's Black Hills Gold
SOUTH DAKOTA MAGAZINE

judge to rule that Black Hills Gold jewelry must be crafted in the Black Hills of South Dakota.

Wasichus were brazen enough to kick it off, but today people of all colors are crazy about Black Hills Gold jewelry.

Wild Horse Harry Hardin was a colorful figure-head for Landstrom's Black Hills Gold.
SOUTH DAKOTA MAGAZINE

★ ★

Who Wrote "The Cowboy's Prayer"?
Custer State Park

Most rodeo fans don't know who wrote "The Cowboy's Prayer," a popular poem often read before the bucking begins. It's usually attributed to some feller named Anonymous. But some cowboys and English teachers in South Dakota know that it was penned by Badger Clark, the literary lion of Custer State Park in the 1940s and 1950s.

Clark himself even joked that his pen name was Anonymous. He never became perturbed at the literary slight, even when "The Cowboy's Prayer" became his best-known work.

Today you can tour the eccentric writer's cabin in Custer State Park. The Badger Hole, near Legion Lake, is exactly as it was when Badger died in 1957. His boots are by the bed, and his old Smith & Corona typewriter seems ready to accept another poem.

Notice the yellow lines on Badger's steps? He painted them so he wouldn't trip when he came home after dark. The first and last steps have wider stripes. Other cabin dwellers in the mountains continue the tradition.

Relatives and fans of the late poet operate the Badger Clark Memorial Society. Visit the group's Web site at www.badgerclark.org.

The Cowboy's Prayer (excerpts from)

O Lord,
I've never lived where churches grow;
I've loved creation better as it stood
That day you finished it, so long ago,
And looked upon your work and called it good.
Just let me live my life as I've begun!
And give me work that's open to the sky;
Make me a partner of the wind and sun,
And I won't ask a life that's soft and high.

Make me as big and open as the plains;
As honest as the horse between my knees;
Clean as the wind that blows behind the rains;
Free as the hawk that circles down the breeze.
Just keep an eye on all that's done and said;
And right me sometimes when I turn aside;
And guide me on the long, dim trail ahead—
That stretches upward toward the Great Divide.

—Badger "Anonymous" Clark

The poet, on the steps of his Badger Hole

★ ★

No Fool's Gold for You

Deadwood

Fool's gold gets no respect, but when Olaf Seim and James Nelson started Broken Boot Mine in 1878, they made more money from fool's gold than the real deal. Fool's gold is actually iron pyrite, which produces sulfuric acid, a chemical necessary in mining camps for processing gold ore.

Thanks to that, Seim and Nelson kept the mine going until 1904. It reopened during World War I for a few years and then closed again until 1954, when Seim's daughter aired out the old tunnels and started a tourist attraction. Today a nonprofit group provides tours, and kids are invited to pan for gold in a sluice. They always go away with a flake or two of real gold—but the fool's gold is strictly off-limits.

Call (605) 578-1876 for more information on the Broken Boot (you'll find it on Upper Main Street), or dig into www.brokenboot mine.com.

Did Wild Bill Love Calamity Jane?

Deadwood

Did Martha love James? Was it reciprocated? Simple questions, but they've never been answered.

Martha (Calamity Jane) Canary and James Butler (Wild Bill) Hickok lie side by side on Mount Moriah, perhaps the most famous boot-hill cemetery in the West. Moviemakers and romance novelists love to pair the two Deadwood celebrities, but in real life it appears that they were friends at best—until Hickok was shot while holding the dead man's hand (aces and eights) at Saloon No. 10 in Deadwood.

Hickok's reputation grew after his death and so, it seemed, did Calamity's affection for him. Through the years, almost until her own death in 1903, she posed by his grave for photos and told reporters (wrongly) that she played a key role in his killer's trial and hanging.

★ ★

She even claimed, late in life, that she and Hickok were engaged to be married.

Martha asked to be buried by Hickok. Deadwood promoters liked the idea because they thought the storied romance was good for business. Buried near the Romeo and Juliet of the mountains (see, now *we're*

Trivia

In downtown Deadwood, Wild Bill's shooting is reenacted daily at Saloon No. 10, and the trial of his killer, Jack McCall, is replayed every evening except Sunday at 8:30 p.m. Gambling was legalized in 1988; profits have been used to restore Mount Moriah and all the historic spots in Deadwood Gulch. Visit www.deadwood.org or call (605) 578-1876 for more information.

Wild Bill and his cohorts still haunt old Deadwood.
SOUTH DAKOTA TOURISM

★ ★

linking them) are Potato Creek Johnny, Preacher Smith, and hundreds of other lesser-known and better-behaved frontiersmen and women.

Admission to the cemetery (situated on the mountain above town) costs one dollar—one pull of the lever in the gambling town below. Call (800) 999-1876 for information.

Easiest City in America to Have a Museum
Deadwood

Travelers who are bored with the butter churns and horse harnesses of the Midwest's typical prairie museums will want to visit the Adams Museum in Deadwood. As you might surmise, this is an easy city to collect crazy and unusual stuff. Here are just a few examples:

Potato Creek Johnny's gigantic 7¾-ounce gold nugget. Is it the

The nudes look modest in miniature.
ADAMS MUSEUM, DEADWOOD

largest found in the Black Hills, or did he fuse several together?

A 9-foot sandstone sculpture of Wild Bill Hickok that marked his grave at nearby Mount Moriah Cemetery from 1902 until 1955. Souvenir hunters chipped off the head and arms and other bits, so it was finally removed to the museum. Museum staff would like the missing parts if you have them. No questions asked—just walk in the front door with the head in your arms.

A miniature carving of a nudist colony, created by a partially paralyzed night watchman for the Homestake Gold Mine. The self-taught artist carved over a hundred women demonstrating various forms of activity—from dancing and playing ball to reading and contemplating the cosmos.

A fancy fur coat and hat worn by Pam Holliday, one of the town's last brothel madams.

And, naturally, every rural museum should have a two-headed calf. The museum curator keeps it as a reminder that many early American museums began as cabinets of curiosities.

You'll find the Adams Museum at 54 Sherman Street in downtown Deadwood. Call (605) 578-1714 for more information. The Historic Adams House, the museum founder's beautifully restored Victorian mansion, is also open for tours and is located at 22 Van Buren Avenue. Call (605) 578-3724.

Railroaded at the Lucky Nugget
Deadwood

Once upon a time, trains ran everywhere in South Dakota. Most of our towns were planned and platted by railroad officials. Lumber, grain, and livestock industries were built along the tracks. Town kids hung around the local depot to see who might depart the passenger cars.

That culture is disappearing, and most of our depots have been converted to restaurants and offices. So while trains still carry coal and corn through South Dakota, they've lost the magic of yesteryear. Oddly enough, you can get a taste of railroading's glory days in the basement of the Lucky Nugget Gaming Hall (614 Main Street) in Deadwood.

Miniaturized versions of the trains that developed South Dakota—including the CN&W, the BNSF, and the DM&E—run hither and thither on narrow-gauge tracks past farms, ranches, mountains, towns, sawmills, and rock quarries. The trains cross over creeks and rivers and skirt waterfalls.

Tiny plastic people are sightseeing, doing chores, sunbathing, ogling sunbathers, fixing cars, herding cattle, and doing many of the other activities common to South Dakota. It's all at 1/87th scale—a standard for serious modelers. But the dozen old-timers who have been creating the exhibit since 2000 hardly seem serious. Other than their height, wrinkles, and gray hair, they more closely resemble schoolkids at play when they meet on Wednesday and Saturday

Engineering at the Lucky Nugget

mornings to work on the ever-expanding exhibit.

So here's an insider's tip: Visit the exhibit on a Wednesday or Saturday morning, because if you show even a little interest, the "boys" will invite you to join them in the middle of it all. They'll point out scenes that you'd otherwise miss, and reveal the inspiration behind various buildings and settings.

Get a glimpse of the exhibit at www.nhrailwaysociety.org if you can't travel to the Lucky Nugget anytime soon.

Ghost Boss Haunts Hotel
Deadwood

Guests are safe, but employees of the nineteenth-century Bullock Hotel in Deadwood soon learn to look busy. It seems the ghost of the hotel's founder abhors idleness.

Seth Bullock arrived in Deadwood with the frenzied gold rush of 1876. He became sheriff and cleaned up the lawless camp, bringing at least a pretense of civilization. Bullock, a businessman at heart, erected a building and started a hardware store in 1879. After a fire in 1896, he reopened it as a luxury hotel, the finest in the Black Hills. It had Turkish baths, a restaurant, and a library. The ex-sheriff was a tough taskmaster with the hotel workers.

After Bullock died of cancer in Room 211 in 1919, strange things began to happen at his hotel. The paranormal activity continues today: Lights and appliances switch on and off, noises are heard, and some people have even reported seeing ghostly images of the founder in the halls and rooms. Hotel staffers claim that if they don't stay busy, the ghost boss becomes greatly irritated.

The hotel closed in 1976, but it reopened and enjoyed a great resurgence after gambling was legalized in Deadwood in 1988. It appears Bullock's shenanigans haven't hurt business; in fact, a registry book in the lobby proudly documents ghost stories.

Call (800) 336-1876 to book your haunted room, or visit www .historicbullock.com. See photo on next page.

269

An early, pre-ghost photo of the Bullock Hotel
SOUTH DAKOTA MAGAZINE

Bloodless Buffalo Jump
Deadwood

Several steep drop-offs in western South Dakota were known to Indian hunters as favorite "buffalo jumps." Just as the name suggests, the buffalo unwittingly jumped to their deaths after being chased over cliffs.

This hunting style seems less sporting than the more direct "attack by horseback" method as realistically portrayed in the movie *Dances with Wolves*. But jumps required less time, trouble, and arrows—and it was much safer (for the hunters) because buffalo are vicious when threatened. In the movie, Lieutenant Dunbar (Kevin Costner) and his Indian friends engage in a grueling, bloody, and bruising buffalo

Artist Peggy Detmers's re-creation of a buffalo jump

★ ★

chase. Nobody was hurt in the movie version, though, not even the buffalo.

For an idea of what a buffalo jump was like, visit Tatanka, a cultural center on the outskirts of Deadwood, where a huge hillside sculpture by artist Peggy Detmers shows Indians on horseback chasing buffalo over an actual cliff. Call (605) 584-5678 or visit www .storyofthebison.com for more information.

The Highest Grave Site
Harney Peak

Mathematically speaking, Valentine McGillycuddy traveled a shorter distance to heaven than anyone else buried between the Appalachians and the Rockies.

McGillycuddy was a frontier physician, adventurer, businessman, and reservation administrator. He tended to Crazy Horse in 1877 when the Lakota chief was knifed at Fort Robinson in Nebraska and stayed at the chief's bedside throughout a long and tense night, administering morphine and doing what he could to provide comfort. He also doctored injured Indians after the Wounded Knee Massacre of 1890. Years later, while living in California, an elderly

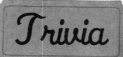

Trivia

Fans of *Dances with Wolves* will enjoy the movie memorabilia at the Midnight Star (677 Main Street) in Deadwood. The restaurant and casino, which is owned by Kevin Costner and his family, has movie posters and costumes from the film.

★ ★

McGillycuddy served victims of the infamous influenza epidemic of 1918.

When he died in 1939, his family received special permission to bury him atop Harney Peak, which at 7,242 feet is considered the highest spot in the United States east of the Rockies, and thus just a little closer to heaven for a pioneer who performed enough good deeds to surely earn entry. And who wouldn't want a shorter trip to the Pearly Gates?

Harney Peak, South Dakota's tallest mountain, is a favorite of hikers.
SOUTH DAKOTA TOURISM

✦ ✦

Trivia

Many people enjoy hiking Harney Peak. Trails begin at Sylvan Lake or Horse Thief Lake. The 6-mile hike is a workout, but it's safe and very scenic. Wear good walking shoes and take water. At the summit you'll find McGillycuddy's grave site, a stone fire lookout tower, and an expansive view of the mountains and prairie. Call the Black Hills National Forest's visitor center at (605) 343-8755 for details.

The $8 Million Dinosaur
Hill City

The biggest dinosaur fight in sixty-five million years erupted during the 1990s around a quiet little museum and research center on Hill City's main street. It's known today as the Black Hills Institute of Geological Research.

The furor began in 1990 when the institute's Sue Hendrickson discovered dinosaur remains near Eagle Butte. Pete Larson, the group's founder, paid the landowner for permission to remove the specimen, which he named Sue. Trouble started as soon as it became apparent that Sue was the biggest T. rex skeleton ever found.

Federal and tribal officials, the landowner, and Larson became legally entangled. FBI agents raided the little Hill City museum in 1992 and removed Sue. Sotheby's later auctioned her for $8.3

million, and in 2000 she became the feature exhibit for the Field Museum of Natural History in Chicago, 900 miles from the hills she roamed in prehistoric South Dakota.

Federal authorities aggressively prosecuted Larson. He was charged with more than a hundred criminal counts, but eventually he was only found guilty of a few minor, unrelated infractions like failing to declare traveler's checks to customs agents. Still, he was sentenced to two years in prison.

Larson and his associates continue to work as fossil hunters. Even though Sue got away, the Black Hills Institute (217 Main Street) has other Jurassic skeletons and exhibits galore. Visitors are welcome, unless you're FBI.

For more information call (605) 574-4289 or visit www.bhigr.com.

A Steamy Movie Star
Hill City

Even though she's aging and heavy and smokes a lot, the steamy star of little Hill City has been in a Steven Spielberg movie and has people climbing all over her every day.

Shame on you! We're talking about Engine No. 7, of course, the 174,000-pound locomotive that provides passenger service between Hill City and Keystone. It's a 10-mile stretch up Tin Mill Hill and across Battle Creek, through some of the Black Hills' most picturesque scenery.

She was built in 1919 and has been pulling the 1880 Train, America's oldest continuously running excursion train, since 1962. The track between the two mountain towns was built in 1888, and two of No. 7's seven passenger cars also date to that era. The bright red caboose was once a drovers' car; in ranching country, drovers loaded their livestock onto the cattle cars and then rode along in the caboose.

Engine No. 7 is one of the country's oldest locomotives, and she gets a lot of attention. You may have seen her in *Gunsmoke, Orphan*

The 1880 Train steams up the Hills.

Train, and *Nick at Night.* But she still gets hot every time she sees a passenger. Call (605) 574–2222 to make a date, or check out www.1800train.com.

Mustangs First, People Second
Hot Springs

Visitors are welcome at Dayton Hyde's Wild Horse Sanctuary, but they come second to the 400 horses. That's at the insistence of Hyde, the old cowboy and writer who takes exception to government programs designed to protect wild horses and other wildlife, but instead put the public ahead of the animals.

Hyde started a nonprofit, private sanctuary and switched the priorities. Some mustangs go unseen for years on his 17,000 acres south of Hot Springs. About 10 percent of the land is open to visitors; the rest is left to the elk, deer, cougars, coyotes, eagles, and, of course, the wild horses. "We've had mares that we've written off as dead come in with a foal at their side, a yearling, and a two-year-old that we haven't seen," Hyde told us.

Ten thousand people visit the ranch each year, knowing they play second fiddle to four-legged freeloaders who have never given a man a ride or pulled one wagon. Hyde appreciates each person; he thinks they can learn from the mustangs, and they help him meet the expenses of running a home for horses that, like Hyde, don't put people first.

Call (800) 252-6652 for information on the Wild Horse Sanctuary (west of Hot Springs on Rocky Ford Road) or visit www.wild mustangs .com.

Some mustangs disappear for years on the huge Wild Horse Sanctuary.
SOUTH DAKOTA TOURISM

★ ★

The Mammoth Site
Hot Springs

Nowhere in the world will you find mammoths alive, of course, and nowhere but Hot Springs will you find dozens of them buried deep in an ancient sinkhole.

Since the archeological site was uncovered in a housing project in 1974, more than fifty mammoths have been found, along with the skeletons of wolves, bears, and coyotes. The mammoths died out an estimated twenty-six millennia ago. The biggest creatures since the dinosaurs, they looked like huge, hairy elephants. Their massive tusks

Excavating the tomb of young male mammoths
SOUTH DAKOTA TOURISM

have been discovered among the skeletons in this Black Hills town.

Archeologists soon realized that they were excavating an ancient sinkhole. Most of the mammoths were young males, leading to speculation that they probably wandered away from the herd and into deep trouble.

The excavation is being done in situ, meaning the bones are revealed but left where they lay. A huge beamed building has been built over the bones. The dig goes on year-round, and visitors are always welcome.

Call (605) 745-6017 or visit www.mammothsite.com for more information.

Hot and Healthy Profits
Hot Springs

Local newspaper editors are sometimes full of hot air, but the *Daily Hot Springs Star* writers put snake oil salesmen to shame when they editorialized on the virtues of their town's naturally warm spring waters.

Lakota Indians called the bubbling springs in the southern Black Hills *Wi-wi-la-kah-tak,* which means "springs hot." They thought the waters had healing powers, but they didn't advertise it. When the town builders showed up, they knew that other American towns blessed with similar springs had capitalized handsomely, so they quickly established hotels and bathhouses to accommodate visitors. The grandest of them all was a sandstone hotel built by Fred Evans, who also constructed a big domed pool for swimmers known as Evans Plunge.

In 1887 the newspaper noted that Mrs. Paddock, the wife of a Nebraska senator, came to Hot Springs in the care of a nurse and within a few months time had made such dramatic progress that the nurse was sent home. "Mrs. Paddock has fully recovered after many years of suffering, a result wholly due to the mineral properties of the Hot Springs water," wrote the *Star* editor.

★ ★

Mrs. Granville Bennett, wife of a Deadwood judge, said the waters relieved her rheumatism. A Woonsocket minister delivered a sermon about a church member's miraculous recovery after bathing in Hot Springs' waters.

Today Evans Plunge is one of the nation's oldest and biggest indoor swimming holes, and the water is still eighty-seven degrees Fahrenheit, winter and summer. The only difference is that the townspeople no longer promise cures for asthma, rheumatism, tuberculosis, or gout. All they guarantee is good, clean fun. But is there anything healthier?

Dive into www.evansplunge.com for pictures and more information, or phone (605) 745-5165. The plunge is on the north side of Hot Springs along SD 385.

Trivia

Got a sweet tooth? Be sure to visit Keystone, a little town with a big main street and lots of candy shops at the foot of Mount Rushmore. Keystone also has fine restaurants, museums, and fun activities like daily gunfights featuring Big Dave Murra, a giant of a man who's known as the Terror of the Rockies. The town took its name from a nineteenth-century gold mine.

Big Dave Murra is a popular "bad guy" in Keystone.
KEYSTONE CHAMBER OF COMMERCE

★ ★

Among America's Most Winding Roads
Keystone

The average South Dakotan likes black coffee, thick steaks, and straight roads. But we make an exception for Iron Mountain Road, one of the most crooked 17 miles you'll ever drive.

Iron Mountain Road is part of a highway trilogy, along with Custer State Park's Wildlife Loop and the Needles Highway. The three together are called the Peter Norbeck Scenic Byway, a route that was proclaimed one of America's top ten scenic drives by the Society of American Travel Writers.

Iron Mountain is one of America's most scenic drives.
SOUTH DAKOTA TOURISM

★ ★

We recommend all three roads (70 miles total), but Iron Mountain is a marvel of both nature and architecture. Peter Norbeck, every learned South Dakotan's favorite politician, helped select the route in 1933 even as Mount Rushmore was being carved.

Norbeck, then a sixty-three-year-old U.S. senator, hiked and rode horseback over Iron Mountain, looking for views that best showed off the Black Hills landscapes and the emerging faces at Rushmore. Others wanted the road to skirt the peak, but Norbeck insisted on beauty over economy. Already in poor health when he was scouting the path, he died just three years later.

His road squeezes through three stone tunnels, spirals down three pigtail bridges, and winds round and round to the 5,445-foot summit, where a small parking lot allows visitors to get out from behind the wheel and enjoy a panoramic view of the mountains, including Mount Rushmore. There at the top, a monument to Norbeck reads HIS WAS THE HERITAGE OF COLD, STRONG LANDS.

Street of Impending Doom
Lead

Lead probably has the world's only Cyanide Street. One symptom of cyanide poisoning is a "feeling of impending doom," but home owners here aren't showing any signs. In fact, they don't even find it unusual. Other streets are called Mill, Miners, Rock, Gold, and Prospect.

The city itself (so named because it sat above the Black Hills' richest "lead," or vein of gold) was a mining town, so Cyanide Street probably didn't seem poisonous to the scientists, engineers, and hard-rock miners who used the chemical in their daily work to extract gold from ore. Four hundred miles of horizontal tunnels were hollowed out beneath the city and surrounding mountains; some are as deep as 8,000 feet.

Today the gold miners are gone, and tourism is the leading industry. Whitewood Creek, once gray with pollution from the mines,

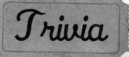

Trivia

When Peter Norbeck asked highway engineer Scovell Johnson if he could build a road through The Needles, Johnson replied that he could "if you can furnish me with enough dynamite." Norbeck, then the governor, scrounged 150,000 pounds of explosives, and today the 14-mile Needles Highway is another stunning, if curvy, drive through the mountains.

has been restored as a trout fishery. We know of a fishing guide at 116 Cyanide Street who advertises, "There's more than gold in our streams!" He has a good slogan, but maybe he should rent a P.O. box and drop the Cyanide Street address from his ads.

Lead is an interesting place to visit, with a mining museum, opera house, art galleries, and other attractions. Call (605) 584-1100 or go to www.leadmethere.org for details.

All the Presidents
Lead

Mount Rushmore honors just four presidents, but all of them are featured 40 miles away at President's Park, the creation of sculptor and painter David Adickes. The wooded, fifty-three-acre complex near Lead has busts of every president. The shortest, James Madison (5 feet 4 inches), and the tallest, Abe Lincoln (6 feet 4 inches), get about the same treatment: All the heads are 16 to 20 feet tall.

Adickes has a sense of humor. His park has a Monica Rock, for example, and the restrooms are labeled "Presidents" and "First Ladies." Our leaders' heads are hollow, but the artist doesn't say if that's a commentary on politics.

★ ★

Honest Abe, the frontiersman, in the Black Hills
JERRY WILSON

President's Park (104 South Galena) is just 5 miles southwest of Lead-Deadwood on US 85. Call (605) 584- 9925 or visit www .presidentspark.com.

Trivia

The Lead Opera House championed by Superintendent Grier was opened in 1914, the year he died. It was a cultural hub of the northern Black Hills for decades before falling into disrepair. Ironically, at the very time the gold mine was closing, the community accomplished a major renovation of the opera house at 309 Main Street. Call (605) 584-2067 for event schedules.

The Black Hills' Best Boss
Lead

Eight-hour workdays were for slackers in the nineteenth century, and holidays were restricted to Christmas and Thanksgiving. But when workers at Homestake Gold Mine asked for a Labor Day holiday in 1888, their boss decided to close the mine; he even provided the company's railroad for picnic excursions. Then he spent the afternoon seeing to the comfort of the riders. The boss was Thomas Grier, and his image is memorialized in granite.

Grier was a young bookkeeper before becoming superintendent of the mine, which was owned by the well-known Hearst family of California. Homestake's Labor Day came six years before the U.S. Congress created a national holiday by the same name.

The Homestake superintendent wasn't a fan of unions. In fact, he fought his workers over the closed shop concept and other issues. But he was dedicated to improving conditions for workers both in the mine and all over town. He encouraged his miners to buy Homestake stock so they would have a nest egg, and he convinced the Hearsts to build a library, bowling alley, swimming pool, kindergarten, store, opera house, and other amenities.

★ ★

The stone image of Lead's well-liked boss

Picking up on a West Coast trend, he reduced the workday from ten hours to eight in 1906 without cutting the daily wage of $3.50. He also prided himself in giving a fair hearing to any grievance.

His thirty-year career as mining superintendent came in an era when America's industrial leaders and their workers were generally at odds, but the 2,500 miners at Homestake developed great respect for their leader. When Grier died in 1914, his workers contributed to the erection of a life-size statue that stands on the town's Main Street to this day.

More Neutrinos Than Money
Lead

Several hundred trillion neutrinos filtered through your body in the time it took you to read this sentence. That's also close to the number of dollars that have already been spent on a mile-deep underground science lab near Lead where neutrinos are being studied. Well, that second sentence is a slight exaggeration, but the first one is true.

The lab is being constructed in the legendary 8,000-foot-deep Homestake Gold Mine. Neutrinos were being studied there even as gold was being dug. Dr. Ray Davis installed the first neutron detectors in 1965, and won the 2002 Nobel Prize in physics for his work.

Neutrinos are subatomic particles created from natural nuclear reactions in the sun. Though tiny and invisible and hardly without mass, they shower down upon the Earth day and night at the speed of light. It's very difficult to detect them aboveground because of interference from cosmic rays.

After gold mining ended at Homestake in 2001, state leaders formed the South Dakota Science and Technology Authority to create a lab that is already fifteen times larger than the next biggest, which is in Japan. One of the planners compared the project to "building several skyscrapers a mile underground."

South Dakotans are historically tight-fisted by nature, but we've really opened our collective wallets to look for something most of us will never see. State legislators budgeted $34 million of taxpayers' dollars, Washington has chipped in, and T. Denny Sanford, the state's megaphilanthropist, gave $70 million. Consequently, the big money pit has been named the Sanford Underground Laboratory.

Everyone (at least all the tightwads in South Dakota) hopes the National Science Foundation will eventually invest another $500 million in the lab because scientists believe neutrinos could teach us all sorts of interesting things about our universe—like the origins of gravitation, the source of energy, how to study minute environments, and how to make South Dakotans spend money.

★ ★

The general public isn't allowed underground, but the Homestake Visitors Center provides trolley tours of the surface. If you think you've seen a neutrino or want to donate a few million dollars, contact the Sanford Underground Laboratory at (605) 722-8650.

Famous Faces
Mount Rushmore

South Dakotans are proud hosts of the world's biggest sculpture, the Shrine to Democracy at Mount Rushmore. It is open 24 hours a day, 365 days a year. The four presidents' faces (Washington, Jefferson, Teddy Roosevelt, and Lincoln) are illuminated every summer night with a special ceremony beginning around 9:00 p.m.

Some Rushmore trivia:

- Each of the hardheads is 60 feet high, small for politicians.

- Washington's nose is 20 feet long—yet he never told a lie.

- Abe's eyes are 11 feet wide. They saw a lot of sadness.

- Cary Grant raced across the faces while escaping from villains in the 1959 movie *North by Northwest*.

- Korczak Ziolkowski, the founder and original sculptor of the nearby Crazy Horse monument, worked briefly on Rushmore.

- Rushmore was blasted, not carved. Over 450,000 tons of rock were dynamited and removed.

- Gutzon Borglum, the chief sculptor, liked the mountain because the granite was smooth grained and it faced the sun all day.

- The memorial isn't finished. Borglum died in 1941 while the war was raging in Europe, so funding and manpower disappeared.

- If you had a long tape measure—and could find their toes—the mountain men would measure 465 feet tall. They'd make a great NBA team, but they'd probably all want to be the captain.

★ ★

- Three million people visit Mount Rushmore every year, which is four times more than live in South Dakota . . . even if we count George, Abe, Tom, and Teddy.

    To reach Mount Rushmore take US 16 west of Rapid City and follow the signs. Call (605) 574-2523 for information or visit www.nps.gov/moru.

America's famous foursome
SOUTH DAKOTA TOURISM

Home of the Jackalopes
Piedmont

Jackalopes are a South Dakota version of the Easter bunny—either you believe or you don't. We're not here to convert you. If real 'lopes do exist, they are nearly extinct. That's why the biggest maker of jackalope head mounts, Jackalope Headquarters in Piedmont, now uses rabbit mounts with small deer antlers to duplicate the look. They do nice work. Only an expert could tell the difference.

Yes, this is all very silly. It makes people laugh and poke fun. That's

Sniffing out a jackalope

exactly why the jackalope has not yet become extinct. Every culture has room for humor.

Jackalope Headquarters supplies head mounts to gift shops throughout the Black Hills region. They produce up to 6,000 jackalope look-alikes annually, and they've never had anyone bring one back and say, "Hey, that's a fake!"

Whooopi Ti Yi Yo
Rapid City

Ever wondered why cowboys sing so well? Rapid City songwriter Hank Harris investigated the mystery and discovered that crooning and yodeling was as useful as roping and riding.

Cows often outnumbered cowboys 200 to 1 on trail rides from Texas to the Dakotas. If the bovines became spooked at night, they might trample anyone and anything in their path. To keep the cows calm and collected, the night watchers would sit in their saddles and sing "Goodbye Old Paint" and other timeless tunes. The cowboys called it "singing to 'em."

Harris's research is fascinating. "I came across a story about a new cowboy who was kept on over the winter at a ranch, while one who had been around a while was let go," he says. "When the foreman was asked why he preferred the new cowboy, he said, 'Well, he can sing.'"

Gene Autry and Roy Rogers yodeled to ranchers' daughters. Once again, Hollywood got the story wrong. Real cowboys crooned for their cows.

Some songs glamorized the cowboy life, but other singers were painfully honest. Here's the chorus of an early song called "The Dreary Black Hills" that you'll never hear in a tourism jingle:

Through hell, rain and snow,
Frozen plumb to the gills,
They call me the orphan
Of the dreary Black Hills.

Hank Harris would've made a great cowhand.

★ ★

With help from the Adams Museum and House of Deadwood, Harris has recorded real cowboy songs in a project he calls the *Deadwood Songbook*. For information on his old-time music, visit www.hankharris.com or telephone the museum at (605) 578-3724.

A Wall to Hate
Rapid City

"Something there is that doesn't love a wall," wrote poet Robert Frost. That certainly applies to the much-despised concrete wall in downtown Rapid City's Memorial Park, just below the Rushmore Plaza Civic Center (444 Mount Rushmore Road North). It is part of the 29-mile Berlin Wall that was torn down in the 1990s.

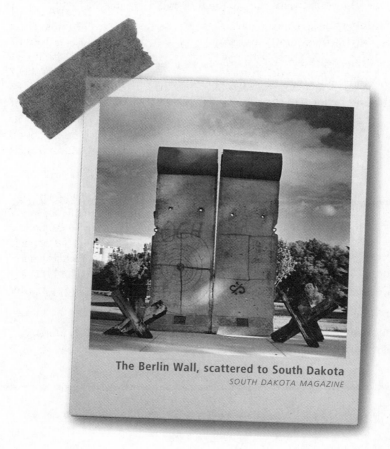

The Berlin Wall, scattered to South Dakota
SOUTH DAKOTA MAGAZINE

Sections of the wall were made available, and Rapid Citians with German connections were able to buy two 13-foot-tall pieces for $450. Shipping the four-ton chunks by ship, rail, and truck to the Black Hills cost another $6,000, but by the time arrangements were made, the same sections of wall were selling for as much as $100,000, so it turned out to be a bargain-basement attraction.

Every president from the 1960s through the 1980s verbally bashed the wall. The most stirring was John F. Kennedy, who in 1963 said, "All free men, wherever they may live, are citizens of Berlin. And therefore, as a free man, I take pride in the words *Ich bin ein Berliner*." Taking a more direct approach, Ronald Reagan said in 1987, "Mr. Gorbachev, tear down this wall!"

Now the wall is scattered all the way to South Dakota. With Mount Rushmore, the Shrine to Democracy, just a few mountains away, Memorial Park seems a fitting place for the stark gray slabs, tombstones to repressive communist regimes.

For more information on Rapid City, the Black Hills' biggest city, visit www.rapidcitychamber.com or call (605) 343-1744.

Trivia

While in Rapid City, enjoy Chinese food at Hunan's Restaurant (1720 Mount Rushmore Road), where you'll also get a visual feast of outdoor photos by Robert Wong, one of the world's great nature photographers. He and his wife, Ying, run the restaurant. When he finds time, Robert takes his camera and heads for Alaska, Africa, China, and other faraway places.

Cadillac of Bulls
Rapid City

One of the lucky mishaps that might befall you on I-90 would be to lose a hubcap near Rapid City, because then you'd likely stop at A&A Auto Salvage and enter the world of "automobilia" art.

While building the salvage yard, Don Gorman dreamed of having a museum of collectible autos and motorcycles in which everything actually worked—and that's just what A&A has grown to become, with the help of his wife, Marsha, and their sons, Dan and Mike.

Autos and motorcycles dating to World War I are on display, along

Dan Gorman and his chrome creation

with toys, bikes, farm tractors, and other collectibles. They're parked around old-fashioned gas stations and shops. Don takes one of the museum's vintage vehicles out for a spin around town every day to make sure there aren't any funny squeaks or tings. The boss can choose his duties.

Visitors are greeted in A&A's front yard by thousands of neatly arranged hubcaps, car seats, grilles, and other auto parts—and by a big shiny bull made of Cadillac bumpers. Dan, a metal sculptor, says it took a year to create.

How many Cadillacs does it take to make a bull? "I didn't count," Dan admits.

A&A's first mission remains used auto parts, but they've happily made room for dad's dream. Find it all at 1525 Seger Drive, northeast of the Rushmore Mall along I-90 (exit 59); call (800) 341-5865. Why wait for a hubcap failure?

"60 Minutes" of Fame for Water
Rapid City

"Doc" Willard was a bona fide scientist who worked on nuclear weaponry and the Manhattan Project before arriving at the South Dakota School of Mines and Technology in the 1940s as a chemistry professor. He loved teaching but he also loved tinkering, so when he retired in 1973, he devoted all his energies toward the refinement of his "super water."

Willard Water is intended to do all the things normal water does—clean, heal, fertilize—only faster. The ingredients are no secret: sodium silicate, calcium chloride, magnesium sulfate, and sulfated castor oil. However, they are combined in a process that polarizes the water and rearranges the molecules.

Harry Reasoner of CBS's *60 Minutes* heard about the South Dakota scientist. In 1980 he gave "Doc" a chance to explain Willard's Water on national television, and sales skyrocketed to almost a million dollars a year. The founder died in 1991 and demand has dropped, but the family-run business in Rapid City still has avid fans and customers who swear by the product.

Some claim it thickens hair, heals wounds, cleans windows and chrome, and even eases arthritis. The Willard family makes no promises. They just keep mixing water at their plant in Rapid City.

The company Web site is www.drwillardswater.com; phone (605) 343-8100.

Hanging Tree Still Standing
Rapid City

Three horse thieves supposedly were lynched on a hill above Rapid City in June 1887. Some local historians believe it was the city's first brush with vigilante justice.

Today the location is known as Hangman's Hill, and Skyline Drive takes visitors past the infamous pine. It died long ago, but the tree's trunk is now fenced and embedded in concrete—a gnarled, gray, wooden reminder of an era when "necktie parties" were the punishment for what today might hardly rate a prison stay.

Horse stealing doesn't carry the stigma it once did, but old ranch families still hate to acknowledge such a dastardly deed in the family tree. One family glossed over Grandpa's thievery and subsequent hanging with this explanation in the county history book: "Grandfather passed away at a public ceremony held in his honor under a big shade tree. Just after a short speech, he tragically fell from his horse and broke his neck."

Fortunately They're Fakes
Rapid City

Seven dinosaurs have stood above the Rapid City skyline since 1936, but even the meat-eating *Tyrannosaurus rex* hasn't caused a lick of trouble.

★ ★

Rapid Citians are accustomed to them, but one grouchy tourist showed up, took a look, and grumbled, "They're fakes!" Thank goodness for that, because if they were real, we'd have to build a very tall fence.

Kids are delighted by what's simply called Dinosaur Park (940 Skyline Drive). The fakes are made of real concrete, so nobody cares if you climb on the back of the stegosaurus or balance on the tail of the apatosaurus. There's also a triceratops, that T. rex, and a few others.

Emmett Sullivan, the designer, worked on Mount Rushmore. Like Rushmore, the dinosaurs were funded through the Depression-era

Prowling the city skyline since the 1930s

Works Project Administration (WPA). Sullivan also designed Dinosaur World in Beaver, Arkansas; the big green dinosaur that welcomes motorists to Wall Drug Store on I-90; and the Christ of the Ozarks in Eureka Springs, Arkansas. That's a decent legacy; Sullivan was no gadfly artist.

The Rapid City dinosaurs were concrete gray until 1960, when they were painted green with white bellies. Maybe that's why the old grouch was very nearly fooled.

Very steep stairs lead from the parking lot to the dinosaurs; this is definitely not wheelchair accessible. Call (605) 343-8687 for more details.

Paper Sculptors
Rapid City

One of the prettiest pieces of art in the American West is just paper. It's a huge snow white scene of a buffalo hunt on display at Prairie Edge Trading Company, a Native American and Old West gallery and store in downtown Rapid City.

Allen and Patty Eckman, husband-wife paper sculptors from Rapid City, spent seven months on the elaborate 7½-by-5-foot three-dimensional scene that depicts a Lakota buffalo hunt and jump on the edge of the prairie in the Black Hills. As five mounted warriors bring down thirteen buffalo, five unsuspecting women and children are caught in the melee. A mother is desperately trying to protect her baby from the falling rocks; the grandmother and granddaughter beckon urgently to a terrified young sister. Details also include startled magpies, petroglyphs carved on cliff walls, buffalo skulls from previous hunts, and much more.

The artists carved the scene in clay, made a mold of the carving, and then used vacuum pressure to fill the mold with their own paper pulp made of cotton and abica. Prairie Edge gallery manager Dan Trimble says the Eckmans' style is unique in the art world. This is their fourth large sculpture portraying life in the West.

★ ★

The Eckmans' *Prairie Edge Hunt* is priced at $55,000. Their small paper sculptures of butterflies, flowers, and feathers are also for sale at the gallery for quite a lot less.

See more Prairie Edge art at www.prairieedge.com or visit the store at 606 Main Street. The phone number is (800) 541-2388.

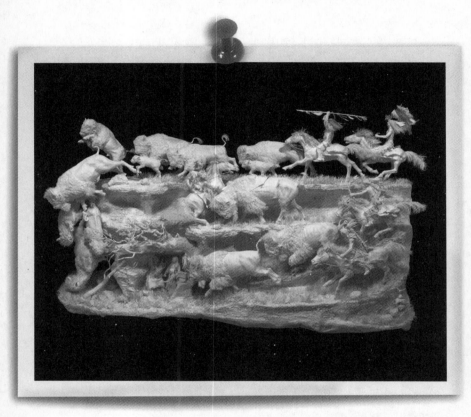

Prairie Edge Hunt **by Patty and Allen Eckman**
PRAIRIE EDGE

Meteorites and Other Worries
Rapid City

The odds of being hit by a meteorite in South Dakota are nearly nil, but proof that it can happen exists at the Museum of Geology on the campus of the South Dakota School of Mines and Technology (501 East St. Joseph Street).

A meteorite arrived in South Dakota in 1956, crashing through the tin roof of a machine shed on a Centerville farm. Both the rock and a chunk of the roof are on exhibit at the museum—along with many other specimens that were detrimentally affected by outer space, since some scientists blame a meteorite for the demise of the dinosaurs sixty-five million years ago. Remains of horrific land and sea creatures have been excavated from the shifting and drifting soils of West River country. More than 19,000 such "finds" have been discovered, and the Museum of Geology has amazing displays of the fossils as well as brief explanations of our geological history.

Mosasaurs, plesiosaurs, and other sea creatures resembling big lizards and sharks were as common as deer and coyotes are today. However, the creatures suddenly disappeared as species, either from a collision between Earth and a gigantic meteorite or due to volcanic activity that suffocated them under several feet of ash. Today archeologists seek their fossilized remains, while kids and amateurs sometimes scour creek beds for inch-long shark teeth that have been washed out of the ash.

The museum is the only place in the world where you'll see ancient, fossilized sea turtle nests. Other exhibits include swimming marine reptiles as long as 30 feet from Frederick, a long-necked plesiosaur from the Salzman Ranch at Iona, a pregnant oreodont, and the complete skeleton of a titanothere.

You'll leave the museum with a better perspective of the fragility of life on Earth. Why worry about painting the garage or trimming the hedges when it might all end tomorrow in a meteorite storm? That's what husbands see when they tour the museum. The odds of any agreement from their wives are equal to the odds of being hit by that meteorite.

For more information contact the museum at (605) 347-2467 or 394-2467.

Never Bitten a Visitor
Rapid City

While working for a small tourist attraction in the Black Hills, Earl Brockelsby noticed that people loved and feared the rattlesnake he kept under his cowboy hat. Hoping to capitalize on man's curiosity, he started Reptile Gardens in 1937.

Brockelsby was right. People do want to experience repulsion. Reptile Gardens is now one of South Dakota's best-known homegrown businesses, perhaps second only to Wall Drug. Still family owned, it is today the largest private collection of reptiles in the world.

The attraction, just south of Rapid City (8955 South US 16), is a mix of science and entertainment. Visitors love the gold-mining pig, the gun-toting rabbit, and the card-playing chicken. They are chagrined when a hen beats them at tic-tac-toe. Kids like to ride Methusaleh, a Galapagos tortoise that is considered the oldest breathing thing on legs in South Dakota. Of course, the true stars at Reptile Gardens are prairie rattlesnakes, cobras, pythons, lizards, and other crawly creatures.

To be honest, there have been about sixty poisonous snakebites and a few crocodile scrapes since the place opened, but never has a visitor been a victim—only staffers, who seem to relish the adventure of working there. Some employees even wrestle the alligators for show. Insurance premiums are high, but that's just part of doing business at Reptile Gardens.

Visit www.reptilegardens.com or call (605) 342-5873 for more information.

Reptile Gardens' Methusaleh, a Galapagos tortoise, was born in 1881.
REPTILE GARDENS

Cosmos: Science or Black Magic?

Rapid City

Is it South Dakota's Stonehenge? A mountaintop Bermuda Triangle? Is the Sphinx pointing this way? Is it a gateway to the Fourth Dimension?

All we really know is that it's weird. At the Cosmos Mystery Area, one of the Black Hills' oldest tourist stops, balls run uphill (and so does water), short people seem taller, and even people with perfect posture can't seem to stand straight.

Are the laws of nature awry, or are they optical illusions? Part of the fun is trying to figure out what's happening to you and those

★ ★

around you. You may not go away with answers to the great questions of the universe, but the Cosmos leaves most people laughing.

English satirist Aubrey Menen believed three things are real: God, human folly, and laughter. "The first two are beyond our comprehension," he wrote, "so we must do what we can with the third." If the Cosmos isn't supported by quantum physics (and who can say?), it still qualifies as real, simply by leaving us laughing.

The Cosmos Mystery Area is located about 16 miles south of Rapid City (24040 Cosmos Road). Visit the site online at www.cosmos mystery area.com or call (605) 343-9802.

Clever Scheme or Mountain Nightmare?
Spearfish

The Thoen Stone looks very old, and it is. The question is whether its message dates to 1877 or 1834.

Brothers Ivan and Louis Thoen claimed to have found the 10-by-8-inch sandstone slab in March 1877 on Lookout Mountain above Spearfish. It evoked an emotional public reaction because of the passionate cursive scribbling:

Came to these hills in 1833
Seven of us DeLacompt, Ezra
Kind, G. W. Wood, T. Brown, R. Kent,
Wm. King, Indian Crow . . . all ded but me
Ezra Kind killed by Indians
beyond the high hill got our gold June 1834
Got all of the gold we
could carry our ponys all got by
the Indians . . . I have lost my gun and
nothing to eat and Indians hunting me.

The two Norwegian farmers displayed the stone at a local store, and then they promptly printed picture postcards and sold them.

Mountain Waterfalls

Thunderhead Falls is underground—600 feet inside a mountain. You hike into the mountain and see the spectacle of Rapid Creek spilling over a 32-foot cliff (10 miles west of Rapid City on SD 44).

Spearfish Falls stopped flowing in 1917 when Little Spearfish Creek was diverted by the Homestake Gold Mine. As mining activity waned, the creek was revived and the falls (a short hike from Savoy) are once again a thing of beauty.

Roughlock Falls, the largest in the Black Hills (also just a nice jaunt from Savoy), took its name from mule skinners who braked their wagons down a nearby steep grade by chaining the wheels. They called it a "roughlock."

Bridal Veil Falls is the best-known Black Hills waterfall because it spills over Spearfish Canyon along US 14A, one of the most scenic drives in America. All around the world, waterfalls have been named Bridal Veil, so we can't claim any originality there.

Spearfish Falls has been revived.
SOUTH DAKOTA TOURISM

★ ★

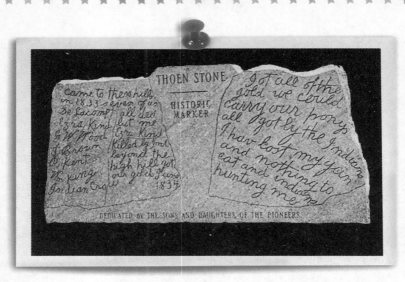

The Thoen Stone
ADAMS MUSEUM

The stone soon became national news, but meanwhile a controversy erupted in Spearfish: Was it really authentic, thus proving there were gold seekers in the Black Hills fifteen years before the big strike in California? Or was it a scam, scratched by the Thoens in 1877?

We still don't know, but an X marks the spot on Lookout Mountain where the farmers said they found it. The stone itself can be seen at the Adams Museum in Deadwood (54 Sherman Street, 605-578-1714). The postcards printed by the Thoens are sold out.

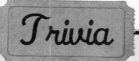

Trivia

Spearfish is a beautiful mountain town, and US 14A through nearby Spearfish Canyon is considered one of America's most scenic drives. For more information on the community, visit www.spearfish chamber.org or call (800) 628-8013.

World-Record Warm-up
Spearfish

An old South Dakotan axiom is "If you don't like the weather, stick around because it'll soon change."

Our climate is highly variable, partly due to our diverse terrain of mountain ranges, river valleys, and plains, and also because North America's cold and warm air masses frequently divide in the sky over our heads.

The world's fastest weather warm-up happened on January 22, 1943, when the temperature at Spearfish rose 49 degrees in less than two minutes—from minus 4 degrees Fahrenheit at 7:30 a.m. to a balmy 45 degrees at 7:32 a.m. It's a record that might not be appreciated in more moderate climes, but Black Hills residents brag about it to this day.

The temperature continued on a roller coaster that same day. It dropped from 55 to minus 5, then fifteen minutes later it rebounded to 55.

An Artist Who Knows No Angles
Spearfish

Ninety-degree angles and Dick Termes never jibed. Termes lives in a round house near Spearfish. He works in a round studio. And his signature art is the Termesphere, art on a suspended globe.

While in college in 1968, Termes decided that since the world isn't flat, there's no reason to always paint it on a flat, square canvas. So he gradually created his own style of painting abstract and realistic images on spheres. He says that if you could be inside the globe, the painting would look like the world around you.

Painting inside-out scenes on a round surface requires some expertise in science, math, and art. Termes describes his method as a six-point perspective. You get a one-point perspective from a standard, flat painting. A compass provides a four-point perspective; Termespheres have that, plus points above and below. "Every line I draw divides the ball in half," he explains, "and every cube I draw projects to all six points."

Termespheres can be found around the world, including a few in South Dakota. *Endless Horizons,* a compilation of 200 Dakota scenes, hangs in the main hall of the Rushmore Plaza Civic Center in Rapid City. *Portholes to the Past,* in Deadwood's old railway depot, shows that city's pioneer history. And *Stairway to Life* is in the lobby of Street Luke's Hospital in Aberdeen.

Dick Termes figures the world isn't flat, so neither is his art.
JERRY WILSON

★ ★

You may also visit the artist's gallery (1920 Christensen Drive), which is located near his home on the southern outskirts of Spearfish. You'll know it by its shape. See his work online at www.terme-spheres.com, or call (888) 642-4805 for more information

How Trout Took to the Tracks
Spearfish

Trout seem at home in the cold mountain streams of the Black Hills, but they were actually introduced in the 1890s by the federal government. Thousands were hatched and raised at the Spearfish fish hatchery, which was started in 1896 along Spearfish Creek.

Today trout are still raised in long, narrow pools surrounded by tidy lawns, stone walls, a rustic wood bridge, and historic buildings. Also on the grounds is a century-old railcar like those used long ago to help the trout make tracks to area waters. Kids can buy small

The D. C. Booth Fish Hatchery has a fish-car exhibit.
SOUTH DAKOTA TOURISM

★ ★

packs of pellets to feed the grateful fish and some very smart ducks that reside at what's now known as the D. C. Booth Historic National Fish Hatchery. Visitors also get an underwater view of a pool filled with large trout. Admission is free.

Black Hills promoters saw a golden opportunity to establish South Dakota as a trout-fishing haven when President Calvin Coolidge vacationed at the State Game Lodge in 1927. The nation's press had naturally followed "Silent Cal" to the mountains, and they were watching his every move. A mile above and below the lodge, workmen strung nets across Squaw Creek. Then they unloaded more than 2,000 big, hungry trout from the Spearfish hatchery into the fenced stream.

Witnesses said that even though Coolidge handled his fishing rod "as gingerly as he might a red-hot poker," he caught five trout in no time. His second outing yielded similar results. Grace Coolidge later remembered Cal "as pleased as a boy with his first pair of red-topped boots." (You may think it's impolite to ridicule the poor fellow for his unwitting role in our ruse, but that's what happens when you live in a fishbowl called the presidency.)

See the fish online at www.fws.gov/dcbooth, or call (605) 642-7730 for more information.

College Basketball's Longest Game
Spearfish

The longest game in NAIA history was played on a cold February night in 1956 at Black Hills State in Spearfish, when the local Yellowjackets beat the Yankton College Greyhounds 80–79 after seven overtimes. It lasted more than three hours, nearly the length of two regular games. Both squads hogged the ball in the five-minute overtimes, hoping to sink shots at the buzzer. The home team won on a free throw after time expired in the seventh overtime.

Since then, rules against stalling and establishment of the three-point line have changed college basketball so much that it's unlikely a game will ever run so long again.

The Original Party House
Sturgis

Hollywood's silly *Animal House* couldn't hold a candle to the simple wood-frame house that once was home to the legendary Poker Alice.

Historians and screenwriters don't agree on exactly who she was— homesteader, Sunday school teacher, card shark, doting mother,

**Poker Alice of old,
and her house today**

311

★ ★

philanthropist, or brothel madam? "All of the above" seems most accurate.

One thing's certain: Alice Tubbs held hellacious parties in her little two-story house. The cigar-chomping mama of seven needed her poker winnings to support the family, and they seldom went hungry. She won as much as $6,000 in a night—and loved every hand. She often said she'd rather play poker than eat a fine meal.

After being widowed thrice and with her beauty and charm fading, she reportedly operated a house of ill repute for soldiers and cowboys. Despite that blemish on her reputation, she's the only South Dakotan ever portrayed by Doris Day in the movies.

Alice's house, while always a curiosity to travelers, fell into disrepair and was about to be destroyed in the 1980s. Local motel owner Ted Walker finally bought it for a dollar and moved it next to the Junction Motel (1802 South Junction Avenue). He'll give tours or even rent you a room. Just a room. Call (605) 347-2506.

Batting for Ted Williams

Sturgis native Carroll Hardy ranks among South Dakota's top athletes. He played in the NFL in the 1950s before becoming a major-league baseball player. His claim to fame? He's the only player to ever pinch-hit for Ted Williams, the greatest hitter in the history of the game. It happened September 20, 1960, after Williams fouled a ball off his knee and left the game. Unfortunately, our hero hit into a double play.

★ ★

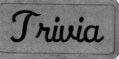

Trivia

Black Hills pioneers, unhappy with the Dakota Territory's leaders in Yankton, attempted to separate and start their own state in the 1870s. Their preferred name was Lincoln. The bill failed in Congress, but Lincoln still got his face on Mount Rushmore sixty years later.

The Biker Belt

Sturgis

Every year in early August, a half million or more motorcyclists roll across America to rendezvous in Sturgis for the world's biggest annual bike rally. They belly up to bars with infamous names like One-Eyed Jack's, Full Throttle, and the Buffalo Chip.

A festival atmosphere permeates the cowboy town of 5,000. Booths and storefronts are stuffed with black T-shirts and leathers, tattoo artists, Harley accessories, food, and refreshments. Bikes gleaming with chrome and metallic colors fill almost every foot of street, leaving a narrow trail just wide enough for two-wheelers.

The Hells Angels are regulars at the Sturgis Bike Rally. Some years their archenemies, the Outlaws, also show and then there can be fireworks. But the rally is usually nothing more than an oversize party of people who live quiet lives during the rest of the year. Most are fun-loving, successful, adventurous patriots. They display the American flag everywhere—on tent tops and halter tops and tattooed in places they would normally keep clothed.

A few years ago, David Horsey of the *Seattle Post-Intelligencer* attended the rally and opined that it's a celebration of America's libertarian streak. Bikers are close to the mainstream of American culture, he wrote. "You won't find biker rallies in Iran or Saudi City

★ ★

or China—only in the USA," concluded Horsey. "To some, a biker rally may look like the end of American civilization, but for better or worse, it may just be the gaudiest expression of who we are."

Make your own conclusions. For more information on the rally, visit www.sturgis-sd.org or call (605) 347-2556.

The rally: a celebration of libertarianism?
SOUTH DAKOTA TOURISM

Mountain Ghost Towns

They always built the cemetery on a point of rocky ground. Some say it was to get the departed nearer to Heaven, and probably many of them needed all the help they could get.

—Hugh K. Lambert and Watson Parker
in *Ghost Towns of the Black Hills*

Ghost towns are everywhere in the West. Before the invention of the automobile, Dakotans wanted a town within a half-day's horse ride. In the Black Hills, camps and towns sprang up in every valley where gold was suspected to be. Many towns were deserted as soon as a better strike was discovered, but others lasted for decades as the townspeople tried to diversify into logging, ranching, or tourism.

Hundreds of town sites have disappeared, while log buildings, gravestones, rock foundations, mining shacks, and mill remnants remain in others. "It has been said," wrote Black Hills historian Martha Linde, "that there is a place on a small hill overlooking the Spokane Mine where on a moonlit night . . . you can hear the faint sound of the miners working with picks hitting rocks."

Ghost towns on public lands are open to hardy hikers with good walking shoes and a compass who know how to read a map or follow a GPS. Watson Parker and Hugh K. Lambert explored such towns as children and later co-authored the well-respected (and recently updated) tome *Black Hills Ghost Towns*. "Ghosts of the past are where you find them," they wrote.

Online researchers might visit www.usgennet.org/usa/sd/topic/ghost for good references. Here are some favorite haunts:

Cascade (7 miles west of Hot Springs) trumpeted its hot mineral waters and became a resort town with substantial sandstone buildings, including a four-story hotel. Today a few buildings remain; others were dismantled and the stones were reused in Hot Springs. Cascade Falls is still a popular swimming hole for locals.   *(Continued on next page)*

Mountain Ghost Towns

(Continued from previous page)

Myersville (near Rochford in Pennington County) has a few decaying buildings and the grave sites of seven miners who died together at the D Mine and of several children who perished in a 1901 epidemic.

Gayville (2 miles above Deadwood) was founded in the opening days of the 1876 gold rush. When nearly all of its 200 houses burned to the ground in 1877, it was rebuilt in thirty days. Town co-founder William Gay was sent to prison for three years for killing a boy who delivered a flirtatious letter to his wife.

Spokane (in Custer County) once had 2,000 residents; traces of the old Spokane Mine can still be found in the forest.

Terry (7 miles west of Lead) is where Calamity Jane reportedly died on August 1, 1903.

Potato Town (in Lawrence County on Potato Gulch) was home to Potato Creek Johnny, a Welsh miner who supposedly found one of the biggest nuggets in the Black Hills. A colorful storyteller who dressed the part, he became popular with tourists as an old man in the 1930s.

Hugh Lambert and Watson Parker co-wrote the book on ghost towns.
SOUTH DAKOTA MAGAZINE

Trivia

Francis Scott Key's "Star Spangled Banner" was the official song of Fort Meade in Sturgis beginning in 1892, long before it was adopted as the national anthem in 1931. Today you can walk the historic square where soldiers paraded to the old tune.

Sturgis was nicknamed Scooptown early in its history by Fort Meade soldiers who felt the town's merchants were intent on "scooping up" all their wages. Today the high school athletic teams are called the Scoopers.

index

index

index

index

index

index

index

about the author

Bernie Hunhoff was born and raised on a Yankton County farm, one
of eight brothers. In 1985 he started *South Dakota Magazine* because
he wanted to stay in his home state and he couldn't find a job he liked.
After more than twenty-five years of exploring main streets, back roads,
river valleys, and mountains, he's been stranded in gumbo, hissed at by
rattlesnakes, mistaken for an IRS agent, and chased in a wild-cow milk-
ing contest. Still, his enthusiasm for South Dakota never wanes.

Over the years he has been involved in newspapering, historic preservation, politics, conservation, agriculture, and economic development.
He has coauthored two other books—*Uniquely South Dakota* and *South
Dakota's Best Stories*—and provided photography and editorial assistance for several others.

He and his wife, Myrna, have two adult children, Chris and Katie.
The entire Hunhoff clan live in the Yankton area.